T0198643

THE KEY
TO YOUR HAPPINESS

A methodology to be *Happy*

MA PREM BHAMA

BALBOA.
PRESS
A DIVISION OF HAY HOUSE

Author Credits: Ma Prem Bhama, Certified Heal Your Life Coach this book shares her experiences and how you can free yourself from pain and suffering. Through this method you can find the way to happiness if you are willing to.

Steps One & Two of the Twelve Steps of A.A. are reprinted with permission of A.A. World Services, Inc.

e-mail address: maprem52@gmail.com
web: www.llavedetufelicidad.com

For talks and workshops: Ma Prem Bhama (787) 722-5212

Editing: Yoga Sanjeeda (Gizelle Borrero)
Divinas Letras (Literatura para sanar)
English Translation: Utte Spengler
Text correction: Clara Fuentes
Design and assembly: Milagros Leblanc
Printing: Impresos de Papel, Inc.
San Juan, Puerto Rico
Photos of the author: Ángel "Cuquito" Peña
Makeup: Cindy Torres
courtesy of Angelo Alberti

Art of Mandala para la transformación: Carlos Díaz

Balboa Press books may be ordered through booksellers or by contacting:

Balboa Press
A Division of Hay House
1663 Liberty Drive
Bloomington, IN 47403
www.balboapress.com
1 (877) 407-4847

Print information available on the last page.

ISBN: 978-1-5043-3509-6 (sc)
ISBN: 978-1-5043-3511-9 (hc)
ISBN: 978-1-5043-3510-2 (e)

Library of Congress Control Number: 2015910212

Balboa Press rev. date: 08/31/2015

Contents

MA PREM BHAMA
(Evelyn Figueroa)

Ma Prem Bhama, spiritual name she was given in 1993 by the enlightened master Osho, was certified as Doctor in Holistic Medicine by the Clayton School of Holistic Medicine under the tutelage of spiritual master Shanti Ragyi. Ever since, she has dedicated herself to help people achieving happiness through therapeutic massages and a renewing concept of spiritual healing she created in 2000 and into which she integrated her knowledge of yoga together with her experience in reading tarot.

She called this self-realization and internal healing methodology Yoga-Tarot for Transformation. After being certified as Life Empowerment Coach in 2006, she incorporated Coaching techniques into this system. She also created a fusion of positive affirmation, visualization and creative writing within her therapeutic mission.

During the last two decades she has been strengthening her formal studies in Holistic Medicine, Therapeutic Massages, Yoga, Tai Chi and Chi Kung attending seminars. (Spirituality and Healing, Harvard University), workshops and initiations with some of the worldwide best known spiritual masters, writers and Yoga teachers like His Holiness the Dalai Lama, Louise Hay, Chris Griscom, Nishala Devi, Debbie Ford, Cheryl Richardson, Brian Weiss, Pete Sanders, Carolyn Myss, Iyanla Vanzant, Rodney Yee, Shiva Rea, Patabi Jois, Don Miguel Ruiz and Wayne Dyer, among others.

In 2012 and 2013 she was certified as a Heal your Life Coach and Leader by Patricia Crane and Rick Nichols, founders of Heart Inspired presentations. *Heart Inspired Presentations is a safe, gentle, loving hub for motivational, inspirational ideas to help you discover your true self, your life's purpose, and your natural goals for success* based on the philosophy of Louise L. Hay.

REMINDERS

The names of the people in the stories told in this book have been changed in order to protect my clients' privacy.

If you do not practice Hatha Yoga regularly, remember to do the easy pose.

While doing the poses, remember to breathe deeply at every moment.

This method is not a substitute for a medical or mental health professional treatment.

For all the

Beings of Light

of the

Three Times

COMING TO KNOW
THE KEY TO YOUR HAPPINESS

By Shanti Ragyi

When I finished reading the book *The key to your happiness* written by Evelyn Figueroa, also known by her iniciatic spiritual name, Ma Prem Bhama, I felt a great admiration for her capacity to explain, recreate and document her internal self-healing and recuperation process. Her book is the best proof of the scope and depth of her authentic transformation and even more.

In her writings Ma Prem Bhama invites us to go on a journey to share the teachings that made it possible for her to find the key to her happiness. She offers us the findings of this access in a clear and specially detailed vision of those techniques and methods that define her process of self-knowledge. They highlight the study of yoga science combined with its practice and the reading and reflection of Tarot as a tool to achieve the connection with the inner self.

The author has found her happiness-center, and through her book she wants to invite the readers to enjoy this internal satisfaction. Her soul desires that others too can feel the pleasure of living fully by sharing this publication.

In its contents, the book gives us the opportunity to get to know powerful techniques like reflexive writing, to recognize our ability to identify and discover the immense power we have to heal and obtain the greatest satisfaction by effectively relating to all aspects of our life.

What a beautiful present her generous heart gives us through her sincere testimony of liberation from pain and suffering from all limiting experiences attached to the past! Through her stories, Bhama shares her meetings with spiritual masters of different times and tendencies. Being an experienced spiritual seeker, she gives great confidence to new readers who are about to be initiated on the path of self-realization.

The key to your happiness is an excellent self-help work. It makes it possible for her to guide you through this process, and you can be sure to find your happiness much faster than you imagine. There are many ways to access Dharma, or the state of total realization, and this is only one of them. Thank you Bhama!

ACKNOWLEDGEMENTS

If this were your first book and you had to write acknowledgements, whom would you acknowledge? How many people would you like to thank for having accompanied you in this adventure? How would you start?

What I consider the beginning......the Divine Energy of the Universe. That is the way I am going to begin. Thanking this Divine Energy, this Universal Mind, this Superior Being, the Protective Forces of the Universe (Shoten Zenllin), what many call God, who guided me at every moment. Every word, every way to express myself have been transmitted to me by Him-Her. When there were moments when I did not know how to address a topic, I would close my eyes, ask for an answer, and there it was immediately. I thank and appreciate the Universe for my having been ready, because "when the student is ready, the teacher appears". I give the most infinite thanks to my Beloved, the unconditional support, for being always at my side.

I also want to thank the Protective Forces of the Universe, the parents and the family given to me and which I chose. With them I continue to learn the virtue of humility. Daddy is already back to his origin, and Mommy continues to give me lessons of humility, perseverance and great patience. Thanks to my brother and all his family. To my nephews and grandnephews who are my greatest teachers; I thank them infinitely for everything they taught me.

I appreciate and thank Shanti Ragyi my beloved teacher, to whom I owe my new life. My beloved teacher who I think is illuminated. Without all those paths, teachings, Teachers, authors, workshops, books and spiritual growth experiences she introduced me to, this work would not have been possible. Thank you for having taken me by the hand and helping me to get back on my feet when I thought I could not start over ever again. There are no words in the entire Universe to express my gratitude and everything I learned.

Thanks to Azucena Gomez, who trained me in the marvelous world of Tarot. Thank you, beloved teacher, back at your origin, for all your teachings.

Thanks to all my friends and companions on the path. Sarita, whom I call one of my yoga teachers and who helped me with the description of the Asanas (Poses), thanks to the support and coaching during this whole process. Yakeen, thank you for your beautiful, always present smile. To Yoga Sanjeeda (Gizelle Borrero) for showing me a new world, taking me by the hand and making me remember that all of us are able to write; I thank her for her patience, perseverance and excellent recommendations. To Lilly García who at a certain moment helped me to reconnect with the Dharma (teachings). To Bebe López who has been an unconditional teacher. To Norma Borges and the newspaper El Nuevo Día for the opportunity and experience of working with them; and my favorite pilot Javier Elías, who taught me the terms and mechanics of planes. To my Tai Chi and Chi Kung teacher Héctor Pozo, for his patience and perseverance in teaching me the synchronized movements of these millennial arts. To my "spiritual soul mates" for helping me to keep my feet on the ground: Fifi, Carla, Ivonne, Neyda and Nydia. To my childhood friend, Lynda Morán, for taking me by the hand through the buddhist teachings of Nichiren Daichoni.

Apart from that, I would like to specially thank Rob and Trish MacGregor, who were kind enough to allow me to get inspiration from their book *The Lotus and the Stars,* in order to define the yoga poses to be practiced in each area. I learned from them that: *there* is nothing new under the sun, everything that seems new is simply a redefinition of what has already been done.

I also want to thank the rest of the "crowd" who are so many that another book would be needed to mention all of them; but as it says in many books I read: "you know who you are".

Namasté

Bhama

INTRODUCTION

The fact that this book is in your hands can be due to several reasons. One of them could be curiosity, or maybe you think that is it a "hocus-pocus" that will give you instant happiness, health, abundance and prosperity.. Or it could be a pill, a magic wand or a fast remedy.

However, I would like to tell you that this book is an instrument for you to work on letting go of things you do not want in your life anymore and to change what does not give you any satisfaction.

What is Yoga – Tarot for Transformation?

It is "The Key to your happiness". An integrated method which makes it possible for you to evolve your life. With this method you are going to use the instruments of Meditation, The Mandala for Transformation, Yoga, Tarot, Meditative Coaching, Meditative Writing (writing in your Journal), Affirmations, Visualization and Action. This book is for people who want to take the reins of their life in their own hands and transform it. It is for the one who wants to work for his/her health and prosperity, find the ideal partner and live the life of his/her dreams.

On these pages I will use the gender She or He indistinctly because the Universe does not have genders, we are energy. We are Ying (feminine energy) and Yang (male energy).

With Yoga –Tarot for Transformation you will apply all your instruments in a systematic and integrated way, and you will keep a journal where you will keep and celebrate your progress. You will also use the Mandala for Transformation, a visual instrument where you will see how you will ascend to reach your goal and how your energy is.

Yoga – Tarot for Transformation will help you to activate the Divine Energy of the Universe, the God in you, the Buddhist nature inside you, in this being of light that you are.... because independently from the spiritual path you have chosen, love does not make exceptions, it does not condemn or judge.

In this journey you are going to embark on, it is recommended to do exercises and tasks that help you to reinvent and rediscover yourself and to remind you that you are a Being of Light with infinite possibilities. This book will help you to recognize that you can achieve everything if you work at it consistently, with faith and let go of being dependent on the results.

MY NOVEL

One day, when I was at the supermarket standing in line, one of the ladies in front of me told another that all of us have our novel, meaning that we all have our personal story. I want to share with you a little bit of my novel, so you can see that when we trust the Divine presence of the Universe always acting in our lives, everything will reveal itself before our eyes.

In one of the "I can do it" workshops taking place in Las Vegas, I heard Iyanla Vanzant (US author and motivator) say that we have to tell our story. When we do that, we let go of much of the destructive baggage we are carrying around. When we share our pain, the load gets less heavy. If we do not tell our story, many times we do not notice the path of healing we have travelled. That is why I want to share my novel with you.

And …..how did I get here to share with you the fact that there is a way that could help you to change your life? When I tried to transform my life, I discovered that I am neither my body, nor the position I hold in an organization, neither a car or what I own; I am a state of consciousness independent of what is around it. I have also learned from Buddhism (in the Tibetan one, as well as in Nichiren Daishonin) and in Yoga, that we are all connected and that everything we do affects our life and our environment. I assimilated that life is marvelous if we want it to be. I learned that, as Wayne Dyer, US author and inspirator says: *If you change the way of looking at things, the things you look at change."* As Shakyamuni Buda said, everything is in the mind. If we change our way of thinking and learn how to meditate, if we do our spiritual practice (anyone we have chosen), and if we analyze the events that happen in our life, everything will change little by little.

Why do I know that this will work? Because I lived it. I have gotten out of the darkness of drugs and addiction. I have gotten out of an abusive relationship where my self-esteem was badly damaged. Sadly I thought that if I left the man who was abusing me, my life would be over. Deep inside me - and without me acknowledging it - I thought that I did not deserve anything better, and that life was only pain and suffering.

After hundreds of attempts to stop taking drugs and tired of telling myself over and over again that *"this is the last time, I am not going to do it again, I am in control and I can stop whenever I want"*, I felt that I could not cope anymore and that I did not want to continue like this.

At one Christmas time, my brother told me that I needed help. I could not believe it, I, who "was always in control"! That first day of the new year I decided to stay at home and not to go out, not to see anybody. I cried and I asked God to help me: only He could do it (first and second step of Alcoholics Anonymous: Recognizing that our life has become unmanageable and that only a superior power could help us).

I stayed locked in my home for seven days, praying and asking God to help me to get out of the hell I was living in. At the end of the week I felt that something had changed inside me, that God had heard me. I felt the greatness of God's Grace revealed in my life. That Divine Energy that sustained me at that time has continued to manifest and show itself to me, opening like a book, giving me a message of my life story on each page, and for this I will be Eternally Thankful. God's Grace sustained me and I was reborn into a new life.

Nevertheless, I will tell you responsibly that if you have an addiction problem, you have to seek the help of a professional.

My case is one of very few where it was possible to get rid of drug addiction by oneself.

I can attest that the Universal Energy (or God) has taken me by the hand and has always protected me. The situation mentioned was one of many quantum leaps in my life, together with a series of happenings occurring one by one, by one. Doors opened and events happened which I did not notice at the beginning. Now I look back and I know that all of them were the best that could have happened to me —even if they were painful for my ego.

Years later something happened that echoed the saying: *"The teacher appears when the student is ready"*. I had a very strong bronchitis and I was watching a program by Cristina Saralegui, moderator and host of "El Show de Cristina", and there was a woman giving her testimony how she had cured her cancer.

Later her facilitator explained how the healing process had been and how the body-mind connection had been used to heal this wonderful woman who looked very healthy. At the end of the program they put the telephone numbers on the screen and I was surprised to discover that this woman lived in Puerto Rico. I called the number the next day and on July 25,1991 (after having seen several analysts, psychologists, etc.) Shanti Ragyi, who became my beloved yoga, massage and mystical arts teacher, received me. That day my life changed and I can say that I was reborn.

At the beginning I filled out a questionnaire of about 50 questions, and later ... the acid test. *"Stand in front of the mirror",* Shanti told me *"and repeat: I love and accept myself the way I am."* That was the moment when things got serious. My God, what have I gotten myself into, I thought. And I heard her sweet and melodious voice telling me: *"Say it aloud so one can hear you: I love and accept myself the way I am"*. So I started (very low, I barely heard myself) saying: I love accept myself the way I am. *"Louder, so one can hear you."* I love and accept myself the way I am. Oh my God! Well, after all it does not sound so bad, it feels nice to love and accept oneself;

and at the end I finished saying it in a loud and strong voice. I LOVE AND ACCEPT MYSELF THE WAY I AM.

This was another big quantum leap. From this moment on I started to appreciate and love myself the way I am. I understand that I am on planet Earth (in Samsara: unending cycle of being born, dying and being born again) and that I have not been illuminated yet, but that I am striving to do so. I accept my virtues and I make an effort to improve and change what I want to change. I admit that walking is step by step, as Lao Tsu in The Tao Te Ching says: "*the journey of 10.000 leagues starts with one single step*". I go little by little, and I pardon myself when I do something which I understand does not agree with the ethics I have chosen to live by, and I take action to correct what has to be corrected.

There have been many quantum leaps during my life, always jumping into the unknown, but being sure that something greater than myself is always there to support me. I am a Catholic, a new awakening Christian, yoga teacher and a Tibetan Buddhism, Tai Chi and Nichiren Daishonin's Buddhism student. All of this in order to come to the understanding that my connection (Yoga) to this force that moves, unites and sustains everything, is individual, because it is between Her/Him and myself. This connection is what has given me peace and serenity and has sustained me during the most challenging moments of my life.

How did Yoga-Tarot come to me? Like everything that has been discovered and which reveals itself to my consciousness; through meditation. One day when Shanti was giving me a massage (I always meditate while she works on my body) I had the idea of combining Yoga and Tarot. I had learned to do an astrological reading with the 22 Mayor Arcanas. Nevertheless, when I looked for an alternative to divination - since personally I do not believe in guessing, because my understanding is that anybody can be his/her own psychic – I asked the Universe what I could do, and the answer was Yoga-Tarot for Transformation.

That is how I started to try this system on myself, and I discovered that it works. As Sarita, one of my yoga teachers, says: *"This works, there is only one requirement, you have to do it."* My first experience was an interview with the newspaper *Primera Hora,* when they called me to do an interview about this new concept; later I was contacted by the newspaper *El Nuevo Día* for another interview. I continued practicing yoga, meditation, affirmation and visualizations, and again God's grace manifested itself in my life. I was called by the editor of the supplement "Por Dentro" which is part of *"El Nuevo Día"*, who asked if I wanted to work with them, and this is how I experienced for myself what it means to put our passion and firm belief to work.

My Superior Being has taken me on marvelous journeys, has opened doors for me up to the point where I am writing this book, which I know is for the benefit for anyone who reads it. I know that it works, there is only one requirement, you have to take action, take up the reins of your life and move the Mandala for Transformation (The Wheel).

Bhama

THE JOURNEY IS FUN
AND WONDERFUL

If we have the love of the partner we have always dreamed about, a job we are passionate about, if our financial situation is successful and if we are healthy, if we are happy with our spiritual path, then we are enjoying a life that everybody wants to live. If on the other hand we go from relationship to relationship, failing in our attempt to create a stable and lasting union; if we think that we do not have what we want, it is time to work on changing what is not working.

If we do not have enough money to pay our expenses, if we are not healthy, if our job does not excite us or create enthusiasm, it is time to take control of our life and to decide to wake up. We are the only ones who can change the things that do not satisfy us.

In order to attract what we want: lasting and satisfactory love-relationships, abundance, a good job and health, it is necessary to work on our change, have fun and be cheerful. Cheerfulness is one of the emotions with the highest vibration frequency, which helps us to connect with the energy of what we want to manifest. Life is wonderful if you put your mind and all your energy to it.

The recommendation is that every day and for the time frame you consider necessary, you make time to honestly answer the questions of the Meditative Coaching section, do the recommended practices for each work area and take action. I have clients who stayed in the Identity area for several weeks and others who stayed only one day. You decide the duration according to the space and

1

energy you have at the moment, it is not important if you do it daily, every two days or each week, the important thing is to do it and make time for yourself; you deserve it.

If you like, read the book completely, or you can start your journey immediately. To do this, choose an area you want to improve and follow the recommendations. Let your intuition guide you. You can go section by section and later you can work with the Mandala for Transformation. Follow the instructions of each chapter. The important thing is to follow your intuition and listen to your inner voice.

The journey you are about to start is fun, and you will discover all the power inside you and how good and wonderful you are.

What are your preferences for the flight? Do you want to go to your destination directly or do you prefer to make stopovers. Sometimes we want to arrive at our destination fast, but Divinity, God, the Universe, or however you want to call it, has better opportunities for you. Maybe God wants you to make several stopovers, because on your journey you are going to meet people who need your knowledge and your love; or maybe God puts angels on your path to help you at that moment when you need it most. As an Anglo – Saxon proverb says: *"Let go and let God"*. Let us always trust that the Universe (God) wants the best for us; so we let things go.

Before you start, get everything you are going to need: your journal, Tarot, your yoga mat and the music you like to listen to, because this journey consists of various stopovers.

The order I recommend is: Yoga, Tarot, Meditative Coaching, Meditative Writing (Journal), Affirmations, Visualization and Action. However, I would like to emphasize that you should always use your intuition and follow the order which you feel is right for you at a given moment.

MEDITATION

Before starting to work on each area meditate at least 10 to 15 minutes. At the beginning of your journey you can meditate five minutes and keep adding minutes until you reach the suggested time.

MANDALA FOR TRANSFORMATION

Work with your Mandala according to the instructions on pages 10, 11 and 12. Keep it close because you are going to see how the energy moves and changes according to your needs at that moment. The recommendation is that after working on the area you chose and after doing the assigned tasks (you have to do this for 21 days at least) you check the Mandala again to see how your energy has increased.

YOGA

A specific pose for each area to work on is recommended. If you do not practice Hatha Yoga you can do the alternate poses suggested for non practitioners, or just sit comfortably. Put your hands on your knees, palms upward.

TAROT

In this book there are two ways to work with Tarot. The first way or spreading the cards is to pick the area with the lowest energy you were able to identify in the Mandala for Transformation and which you want to change. Shuffle the cards and take one, paying attention to the area you chose. Always, before you spread the cards, it is necessary to meditate for a minimum of ten minutes. Then spread the cards using your heart hand (left) and choose one card. Look for its meaning in the Tarot area.

The second way is the Mandala spread. Here you are going to take out one card for each Mandala area. If you like to go according to the Mandala order pick a card starting with area one and continue with the rest of the areas. If you like your intuition to guide you, observe the areas and their names, pick a card randomly, and without looking at it, put if face down where you feel your energy directs you. Use the hand of the heart (left) each time you draw a card. When you are finished, start turning over each area, look for the meaning of each card and apply it according to your own situation.

MEDITATIVE COACHING

Answer the questions of MeditativeCoaching honestly and ask yourself what small big step you can take to increase an energy level in the Mandala for Transformation.

THE JOURNAL (MEDITATIVE WRITING)

Buy a journal so you can keep record of your progress. In it you will answer the Meditative Coaching questions. Write all that comes to mind without judging. Reflect about your answers and analyze them. What things do you want to improve?

In order to move up one level on the wheel you can look for one of the answers to the questions, work on it and take the necessary action according to what you decided to improve in your life.

AFFIRMATIONS

An affirmation is a decree of something you want to happen. When we use our words in a loving way, the Universe manifests itself in our lives responding to the high energy vibration of love. Sing, write, dance and speak your affirmations out loud.

When you affirm that life is wonderful, that only the best is going to happen, that everything is perfect in your world, the energy will move towards these affirmations and everything you said, thought, wrote, danced or sung will manifest itself in your life.

VISUALIZATIONS

Use visualizations to see yourself reaching the goal or goals you have set for each area. If you choose to work with abundance, visualize yourself prosperous, helping others and reaching your objectives.

MIRROR WORK

Five years have passed already since this book was first published in Spanish and where I mentioned the mirror work instrument briefly. However, in this English edition I would like to elaborate on this work because I have experienced it as a fundamental part of my healing process. Every day when I get up the first thing I do is look at myself in the mirror and say: "I love and accept myself the way I am," As a Heal your Life Coach – coaching based on Louise L. Hay's philosophy- I learned that if we look at ourselves in the mirror all judgments and prejudices we have about ourselves come out, like: I am old, I am ugly, I am fat, I don't get anything right, I am a disaster.

However if we practice the technique daily, a slow transformation begins where judgment changes to joy and acceptance, which empowers us to change what we do not need in our lives anymore. We learn to address ourselves in a loving way and when we tell ourselves: "I love myself the way I am" we do it with joy and elation. The freedom you feel at this moment is incredible because you understand that you have broken all the chains that constrained you and transformed them to: I am beautiful, my body is at its right weight, everything is going to happen according to the Divine Plan of the Universe and I accept it. Everything is well in my world. According to my personal experience I understand that when I look myself in the eyes I am sending a message to my subconscious mind, reprogramming it with powerful messages that make me manifest all my goals and desires.

Mirror Work Techniques

There are several ways to practice Mirror Work: One among the ones I like best is to stand in Mountain Pose in front of a mirror where I can see my whole body. I stand firm, look myself into the eyes and say: "I love and accept myself the way I am. I am an excellent and extraordinary Heal Your Life Coach and Leader." I continue to repeat my affirmations at least for fifteen minutes, then I rest and write any low vibration message that came to my mind into my journal with an affirmation regarding that limiting belief next to it.

Another way of doing mirror work is taking a small mirror where you can see your face completely and follow the same proceedings: look yourself in the eyes, smile and say your favorite affirmation. For example: "I love life and life loves me" (one of Louise L. Hay's favorite affirmations). I am peace, I am love, I am forgiveness, I am compassion. Money manifests itself in my life easily in known and unknown ways.

When you practice Mirror Work–every day–there will be a moment when wherever you see your reflection you look at it and what comes out of your mouth are words of encouragement and inspiration for yourself.

At this very intimate time when you are in front of the mirror is your moment of power; take advantage of it and make your affirmations in front of the mirror and you will see how they start to manifest themselves in your life. For me there is nothing more powerful than this.

ACTION

It is necessary to take action to go up in the Mandala for Transformation. Ask yourself always which small big step you can take to get closer to your goal. Some examples are: open a bank account specially for your retirement or another goal you have planned. The American writer and motivator Napoleon Hill tells us in his book *"Think and grow rich"* that he has confirmed that a consistent saving habit will make us succeed. In each area you will find an example of the action you can take. However it is necessary for you to use your intellect, your intuition and that you also make a good analysis of the action you are going to take in certain circumstances.

THE DURATION OF THE FLIGHT

This trip has a recommended duration of 12 weeks (three months); that means one week to work each area, but remember that you are the one who decides the time it takes.

Always put your intention and action to it, taking one small big step and go on your way little by little until you reach the goal you marked for yourself.

Every journey starts with a small step, then another and so on, until we accomplish our goals. The first and second step (taken from the Alcoholics Anonymous 12 step program) is to admit that *"our life has become ungovernable"* and *"only a superior power can help us"*, and we are going to do what is necessary in order to achieve what we desire.

Always see the fun part of your actions, make your affirmations and visualizations in a relaxed way. You will see how you will activate this inner force in you. The journey is relaxed and fun, do not put any stress to it, because energy will stop flowing, which transforms everything into a challenge. During stress and resistance there can be drawbacks, delays, distractions and things which keep us away from our goal. The key is to be relaxed in a fun way.

PREPARING YOURSELF FOR THE JOURNEY
(Mandala for Transformation)

In order to start on your path of transformation, it is necessary to know where you are and where you want to go.

When you work with the Mandala for Transformation you will have an idea where you are in terms of energy. You will see which area of your life needs to improve. In order to achieve this you are going to use the instruments given in this book. If you notice that everything works well in this area (you marked 8, 9, or 10) you can go to the rest of the areas that need work. After filling out the wheel, keep it in an accessible place because you will update it according to your work on the different areas you want to improve.

Photocopy the Mandala for Transformation (page 20). Look for a quiet and peaceful place. It can be on the beach, in the countryside or in a place like a rainforest; a place where you can connect with nature and with God inside you. All these are energizing options with a lot of high frequency vibration and they are ideal for this purpose.

If you are at your place, disconnect all telephones and make sure not to be interrupted. Before you start, meditate at least 10 or 20 minutes. After meditation take the Mandala for Transformation and draw a circle around the number that best describes your energy and satisfaction in this area, with number one for the lowest and number

10 for the highest satisfaction (check the table for definitions). Then draw a line from circle to circle connecting them; that is how you can determine which area is the one that needs the most energy. The objective is to have all areas more or less at the same energy level (from 8 to 10) so they form a circle or balanced wheel.

In every person's life there are 12 areas in which we dance and flow around during our interaction with all that surrounds us.

They are:

1. Identity
2. Finances/Money
3. Mind
4. Home/Family
5. Creativity/Fun
6. Health
7. Relationships: Intimate (love)/social
8. Sexuality
9. Spirituality
10. Work/Profession
11. Goals
12. Introspection

Each area transmits its own energy, influencing the rest of them. If our energy is very low in an area, the others emit their energy to strengthen it. However they get affected because releasing energy debilitates them, which makes it impossible for us to function properly in our surroundings.

For example, if our energy is very low (let's say between 2-3) in the number VIII area, which is Sexuality, usually the area of Finances/Money (nr. II) is going to be affected. Also, if the energy in area nr. III (Mind) is low, all the rest will be affected, because everything is in the mind and it is necessary to work on it immediately.

The areas to take most care of are: Nr. I (Identity), III (Mind), IX (Spirituality) and XII (Introspection). They are the basis that determinates how the rest of the areas in you life are going to be.

The ideal situation is that your energy is high or moderately high in all areas. However if you are satisfied with a moderately high energy in an area and you think that you are content with that, start to work on the others where you marked little or no energy.

Energy scale:

1 – 3	No Energy at all (I feel I am dragging myself, I want to increase my energy because I am not doing well there).
4 - 6	Little Energy (I feel I can more or less function, but I want to be "empowered". The Energy is low, I want to increase it).
6 - 7	Moderate Energy (I feel it is better, but I would like to increase it more, I want to be able to train my mind).
8 - 9	High Energy (Everything works well in this area. I feel happy and accomplished but I would like to reach a 10).
10	Super energized (This area is very good. Everything is the way I want it to be. I feel "empowered and happy").

THE INSTRUMENTS

When a pilot enters the cabin of the plane, he checks if all its instruments are working correctly and that they are the latest in technology to be able to make the trip. He makes sure that anything not useful is removed, that he has a flight plan: the destination where he goes, the distance, the route he is going to take, the gasoline he needs to complete the trip and the existing and prognosticated meteorological conditions in order to take off and reach his destination. He considers alternative routes in case some eventuality happens and he has to alter course. The same thing happens in our lives, many times we trace a trajectory and the Universe puts us on another route. That is why we have to be prepared to change course happily and without reservations.

The pilot uses check-lists in order not to leave out any detail and not to overlook anything. For you the check-list is the Mandala for Transformation.

When you work with it you will use instruments to reconstruct your life, throw out anything you do not need anymore and heal the wounds.

As for any journey, it is necessary to be in an alert and receptive state of mind to trust the pilot. Here you are the pilot and captain of your plane. The more alert and receptive you are, the better your trip will be.

What is necessary for your journey? That you believe it will be successful. What does the word ' to believe' mean? According to the definition in the dictionary of the *Real Academia Española* (Royal

Spanish Academy) ' to believe' means: "*To accept something that cannot be understood, proven or demonstrated as being true.*" So when you start doubting, use it in your favor and look for the answer to your questions. Meditate, analyze and continue on your path until you finish the recommended process. Do not give up.

Sometimes you might feel that the task you are accomplishing is overwhelming. When that happens, laugh. The energy of laughter is very healthy and will help you to confront your fear. There will be moments when you are face to face with your fear, and when you understand that behind the fear there is attachment, you will feel liberated. The process can be fun if you put your mind to it and look at it with joy and enthusiasm.

The word 'enthusiasm' comes from the Greek "enthousiasmos" which means "*it has God inside it*". When you know that the Energy of the Universe lives inside you, you have the necessary strength to correct and reconstruct your life.

First Instrument

MEDITATION

This word has as many meanings as there are teachers on this planet. In this context we will use the definition most closely in tune with fun: to meditate is to relax. In this process we connect with Divinity, the questions we might have will be answered and our mind receives the images we need to reconstruct our lives. Ask and you shall receive.

The undisciplined mind keeps us attached to Samsara (cycle of pain and suffering, continuous rebirth), because it is easier to stay how we are and not take any action and later complain and blame someone else. Not taking any responsibility is the easiest way, blaming others is a way not to take responsibility for what happens to us.

The first big step is to accept that we are the only ones responsible for the events in our life. We create our circumstances and that is the reason why it is necessary to look objectively at what we have created.

There are many meditation techniques. In this process we will use two of them: energetic and relaxed meditation, which will help you to analyze what you have brought to manifestation in your life.

TECHNIQUES
Energetic and Dynamic Meditation

If you are one of the people who say that they cannot just sit down and stay calm, you can do energetic medication. I learned this technique with Shanti Ragyi, my teacher of yoga and other mystical arts. It is a meditation taught to his disciples by Hindu Master Osho, so they could free tensions, fear and anger. In *The Orange Book* this meditation is explained in detail.

A short version (which I have practiced), is turning on the music you like best, preferably music with movement and a lot of energy. It can be drumming, rock, and why not, even reggaeton or hip hop. The technique is to move and move until you get tired. Dance, shake your body, let go of everything you want to get rid of, like: fear, anger, impotency; until you reach catharsis, until your mind gets immersed in what you are doing. Catharsis originates from the Greek word *"Katharsis",* which means purge or purification. When you enter catharsis, you are purifying yourself internally with the help of an exterior *stimulus*, in this case music and movement.

Continue dancing and moving for at least 15 to 20 minutes. Shake your body, twist and turn around and around. Imagine that you are going to get rid of things – which is true, you are freeing yourself from everything you do not want in your life anymore and which is not necessary. Visualize yourself letting go of everything you do not want anymore and make gestures of shedding things. Keep moving until you go into ecstasy –this state of endless love and mystical union with God - lie down on your back on the floor or in your bed and rest for at least 15 minutes with your eyes closed and be attentive to the messages, ideas or images that come to your mind. Pay attention to the answers to your questions, to your connection with the Divine Energy of the Universe. Observe your thoughts and the state of your mind when you start relaxing.

Relaxed Meditation

The Universe gave me the opportunity to attend the "Spirituality and Healing in Medicine" conferences/workshops by the Department of Continuing Education of the Harvard University Medical School in Boston, where the benefits of meditation were widely explained. Dr. Herbert Benson, pioneer in the studies of Meditation benefits, informed that for about 40 years laboratories of the school have conducted systematic studies regarding the interaction of body and mind. They informed that: *"The studies showed that when a person gets immersed in prayer, words, sounds or phrases, physiological changes occur in the body. These changes — lowering of arterial pressure, decrease of metabolic rate and heartbeat among others, - are the opposite of those produced by stress and have been cataloged as the Relaxation Response."*

Dr. Benson explains that many people who obtained the Relaxation Response also increased their spiritual connection and understanding. They expressed spirituality as" *an experience of the presence of a power, a force, an energy, which could be perceived as God. This presence is experienced by the person who feels it closely."* According to Dr. Benson there are two basic steps to obtain *the Relaxation Response*: 1) Repetition of a word, sound, prayer, thought or sentence, or 2) Muscular activity.

When we do these repetitions and a thought comes to mind passively we get rid of it and we get back to repeating what we have chosen until we reach the relaxation response. That leads us to perceive that the train of daily thoughts is interrupted and we experience the relaxation and peace we long for.

While I was studying Tibetan Buddhism, our spiritual master said that meditation (or the Relaxation Response) is the "multi-medicine". When we are in a very challenging situation we meditate; when we are sad we meditate; when we are happy we meditate. We do it for everything, because it has proven to help body and mind.

I feel that when we meditate we feel a Superior Presence that helps, guides and protects us. We feel the presence of something greater than ourselves and we know without a doubt that it is the presence of Loving kindness.

If you feel you are without energy, and you think that everything is over for you, do not weaken …. meditate. Relaxed meditation will give you a starting point to move towards the future, taking into consideration that your moment of power always is in the present. In the present you get rid of the past and build your future.

The undisciplined mind tries to deny the present and run away from it, constantly moving from the past to the future. That creates states of anxiety and confusion, preventing an objective analysis of the true reason of these feelings.

In order to know if you live in the present, ask yourself if there is happiness and enthusiasm in what you are doing. If you do not feel this joy you are entering and exiting the past and the future, and you see life as a continuous effort. Pay attention to what you do and how you do it. Sometimes "why" is more important than "how". Enjoying and being present in the process gives you the needed confidence to totally accept the result. When we trust in God, in Divinity, in the Universe, we know that the result always is for our greater good.

To do the relaxed meditation, if you want, you can put soft music, disconnect all telephones and pick a quiet place where nobody can interrupt you. Light a candle and incense (if you are not allergic to it) lie down or sit comfortably. Put your attention to your breathing and let go of all restlessness; observe your body. Continue breathing. If something comes to mind, let it go softly, do not enter into a dialog with your mind. Keep breathing and focus on it.

When the time you allocated for meditation has passed, open your eyes little by little and consciously observe everything around you. Give thanks for the time and space you have been in Yoga (union) with The Universe.

I also want to share with you a technique how to let go of anger, it is Compassion Meditation. My version of this meditation is easy: breathe deeply and put attention on it. If some thought comes up, softly put your attention back to your respiration. Think of something pleasant and fill your heart with love. Visualize that this love flows over everything around you.

Second Instrument

MANDALA FOR TRANSFORMATION

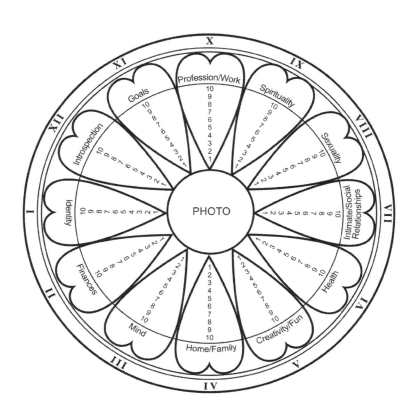

Third Instrument

YOGA

All of us can do Yoga, independently of the way our body is. If it is big, tiny, chubby, skinny, if you are not very flexible, or if you have any kind of disability, you can still do Yoga. After all, the word Yoga means union. Union with Divinity, with God Recognizing that we are one and that we are all made of the same atoms as the last of the stars, we merge with everything that surrounds us. Yoga is not a religion, it does not impose anything on you and it is not competitive. You start where you are and how you are.

There are several types of Yoga, but the four big ones are: Raja Yoga, Bhakti Yoga, Jnana Yoga and Karma Yoga.

1. **Raja Yoga (the Queen of Yogas),** also known as Ashtanga Yoga, is usually attributed to Patanjali, who is said to be the first one to decode this system. His teachings are assembled in the book "The Yoga Sutras of Patanjali" (sutras are prose discourses he taught in India).

    The eight branches or extremities of Raja Yoga are:

    Yama - Correct behavior towards others

    Niyama - Correct behavior towards ourselves

    Asana – Practice of poses (Hatha Yoga)

    Pranayama – Breath control

    Pratyahara - Control of the senses

Dharana – Mental Concentration

Dhyana – Meditation (Samadhi – Self-Realization)

2. **Bhakti Yoga - Yoga of devotion.** It consists of praying, devotional chants, study of scriptures, service. It perceives God – the Universe – in everything.

3. **Jnana Yoga – Yoga of knowledge.** It is based on self –study to take you to self realization, to understand who we are and what our purpose in life is. Jnana Yoga encourages us to continue asking, looking for information and discover what our true beliefs are.

4. **Karma Yoga - Yoga of action.** Our actions are the manifestations of our consciousness of what we believe and think.

If you still think that you do not practice Yoga, think again and reflect. You have done it at some moment. When you sit down to meditate, when you unite your conscience with the consciousness of the Universe and recognize that we are one, at that moment you are doing Yoga; you are in union. Do not get discouraged if you think that you do not know how to do it, you can start doing it on this journey you are going to undertake.

In each working area you will find recommendations regarding which (Hatha Yoga) poses to do to move the necessary energy that helps you to reach your goals.

If you think you cannot do Hatha Yoga, the recommended pose is sitting comfortably to meditate and breathe. That is the way for you to be in Yoga (Union) with Divinity.

The technique:

In each area there will be a suggested pose for the beginners at practicing Hatha Yoga. Do it slowly, paying attention to your body and what it expresses all the time. If you do not feel comfortable doing the pose, let go and return to where you started from.

If you do not practice Hatha Yoga, it is important that you sit on a cushion or on a chair. Always remember to honor your body. If you are not comfortable even in the modify pose, do not force yourself. Simply sit in a Sukhasana (easy pose) or comfortably on a chair, meditate and you will be already in Yoga (Union).

Fourth Instrument

TAROT

What does the word Tarot mean? Many definitions were given, but the dictionary of the Real Academia Española (Royal Spanish Academy) gives the definition as: *"Deck of 78 pictorial cards used for fortune-telling in cartomancy"*.

Others define Tarot as the true path for the knowledge of life. The exact origin of the word is unknown, but many people define it as "torah", which in Hebrew means "law". Other experts indicate that the word comes from the Latin words "rota", wheel; "arot", to work in Greek; "otra', hear from the Greek word otarion; and "taro", destiny with its 22 arcana. Consequently we could say that if we watch the wheel of destiny attentively, we listen to our inner voice, we work on our change and we take control of our life; we could achieve the goals we have promised to ourselves and live the life we have dreamed about.

Nobody knows exactly how and when Tarot came up. According to some scholars it dates back to Ancient Egypt. On the Great Pyramid, drawings were found that resemble the Major Arcana of Tarot, and the story goes that when the priests felt a threat to their knowledge, they decided to draw symbols expressing the wisdom of the book of Thoth (holy book of the ancient Egyptians).

Tarot has been generally used to predict the future. This is not our case. Here we use it as a map that will tell you the journey you choose to undertake.

If you do not have any Tarot cards, acquire a deck of Marsella Tarot. This is the one recommended which I have been using for more than a decade. You could also buy a Rider-Waite deck, which is very well known. Buy the one you are most interested in.

Take out the 22 Major Arcana: The Fool, The Magician, The High Priestess, The Empress, The Emperor, The Pope, The Lovers, The Chariot, Justice, The Hermit, The Wheel of Fortune, Strength, The Hanged Man, Death, Temperance, The Devil, The Tower, The Star, The Moon, The Sun, Judgment, The World, - because it is with them you are going to work.

There are many types of designs of Tarot cards. A deck has 78 cards: 22 Major Arcana and 56 Minor Arcana. Major Arcana are called that way, because many scholars think that in each of the cards there is the history of creation, and they take us to the innermost places of our being to profoundly analyze our life. On the other hand the Minor Arcana deal with everyday life.

According to Dr. Carl Gustav Jung, Swiss psychiatrist and psychologist, the 22 Major Arcana are an illustration of human archetypes and they tell the symbolic history of our internal journey.

Each card is an instrument for this internal journey. When you do the spreading you are connecting with your innermost self, and the message you need will come to you so you can work in this area.

If you made a mark on a number eight, nine or ten and you feel satisfied in this area, but if a transcendental card like : The Fool, The Tower, The Devil or Death comes up, it is necessary for you to meditate and ponder if you are truly as satisfied as you think you are.

In our work we always use the normal position of the card. For me there are no negative cards, only teachings, so if a card comes up flipped, you put it in its normal position so you can analyze it better.

The Spreads

There are several types of spreads. One of the best known is the Celtic Cross, which consists of ten cards in the form of a cross. For our work we use the casting of one card and the Mandala for Transformation. Before you do the spread that you chose, meditate at least 10 to 15 minutes.

In order to pick one card, shuffle them and put them on a table in a half circle. Close your eyes and move the hand of the heart (left) over them. Try to feel their energy vibration and pick the one you feel irradiates energy towards your hand. It is normally perceived as a pleasant heat on the palm of your hand. Look for its meaning and the recommended Yoga pose for the area you want to work on.

If you want to spread Mandala for Transformation©, use the given Mandala and do the same proceedings, taking one card for each area and put it on the Mandala. Look for its meaning in its special section and analyze the message the card has for you.

Fifth Instrument

MEDITATIVE COACHING

When I was studying to become a Life Coach, one of the exercises we were asked to do was to write our own definition of what coaching is. Mine was: *"Coaching is a process that helps people to connect with the best of themselves. It is action oriented and focuses on the present to move the clients forward. It helps them to establish and reach their goals, acknowledging that they has the answers within themselves."*

You have the answers to all your questions, you only have to listen to your inner voice. During Meditative Coaching you are silent, and it is in silence where we hear the answers that our Divinity gives us.

The Universe (God) is always talking to us; it is the mental bustle that keeps us from hearing it. We are on this beautiful planet with all the necessary tools to be happy. But our ego, limiting believes and incorrectly learned things impede it.

Through this instrument we are going to work every area with assigned questions, which have to be answered honestly even if it hurts. Meditation is the basis to get rid of the excess baggage and start our journey to happiness. We are going to find out who we really are. We are going to learn that we are neither only a body or a job, nor a car; we are a state of consciousness connected with Universal energy, even if sometimes we do not notice it.

All of us have personal ways of interpreting events happening in our lives based on previous experiences. We tend to look at life and what happens to us through the lens of the past, without understanding that it is not possible to always act the same way and that the results will not always be the same. There are creative and different ways to do things. We can always choose if we look at our life through the lens of drama or the one of growth.

The goal of Meditative Coaching is to make you see life and its situations through the Divinity that lives within you. Life is wonderful if we intend it to be, if we learn to always see anything that happens is for our benefit, even if at the beginning we do not recognize it that way.

Obviously this is not a substitute for psychology or counseling. It is a personal process where you learn that if you need help, you can look for the sake of your spiritual growth and your emotional and mental improvement.

The Technique

There will be questions in each area and you will answer them honestly and you will write the answers in your journal. Remember they are for yourself, you will not mislead anybody, only yourself if you do not answer them truthfully. In order to see results from this journey, you have to be honest with yourself. This is the basis for energy to move in your favor.

Sixth Instrument

MEDITATIVE WRITING (THE JOURNAL)

From the beginning of human history man has turned to writing as a means of communicating his experiences, knowledge and discoveries. At the beginning drawings were used to depict history, rituals and customs of the time. Later on writing in symbols was developed so that everybody could read it and be informed about what was happening at the moment.

Shanti introduced me to Dr. Ira Progoff, psychologist, creator of the *"Intensive Journal Program"* and student of Dr. Carl Gustav Jung (father of modern psychology). In his book "At a Journal Workshop" Dr. Progoff says that recognizing the problems in our life, observing and describing them as objectively as possible is the first step to work on them. Writing in your journal is looking at situations in a way an observer would. When we make entries in our journal we can do it 'in the third person' which makes it possible for us to get out of the picture in order to see our situation in an impartial way. In meditation we can enter into our innermost self in order to focus our energy on a solution for the challenge or the experience we want to heal.

Additionally, Dr. James Pennebaker, Professor and Chair of Psychology at the University of Texas at Austin, did and is doing studies which evidence the therapeutic power of writing. In his studies he has proven that we use words to transmit our emotions and thoughts to tell stories and understand each other as human beings. Starting in 1980, Dr. Pennebaker and his colleagues discovered that when people write about a traumatic experience during three to four days and around 15 to 30 minutes a day, they show improvement in their physical and mental health.

It has also been shown that writing our emotions can relieve stress and improve physical and mental health. When we talk about traumatic experiences, we let go of an immense burden, which brings about relief and liberation in the process.

How many times did you wish you had a friend who listens to you without judging what you say? How many times have you wanted someone to support you, give you love without expecting anything in return? This friend is your journal, and as part of this system you will keep one, in which you will write down your progress and the recommended tasks. I urge you to work on your journal twice a day, once in the morning and the other one before you go to sleep.

You can buy a binder and decorate it with anything you like: beads, sequins... unleash your creativity! In my case, I bought a binder where I put a division for each area to be worked on (12 divisions), plus one for my internal dialogue and another one to write about and celebrate my achievements, which I call my quantum leaps. That makes a total of 14 divisions.

You can create additional sections and add more, if you think it is necessary. Buy your binder, decorate it and fill it with unlined pages of different colors. You will see how that makes you feel like writing and working on every area of your life. This journal will be an instrument that reflects your existence, your aspirations, your being, your light and your darkness. It will be the instrument where you can put all your emotions. You are going to work each section recognizing your merits and what you want to improve. You journal will be a reflection of your being. Take care of it, love it and keep it entirely to yourself.

The techniques:

Look for a quiet place where you will not be interrupted, and before you start writing in your journal (make your affirmations and write to let go of your emotions), meditate (calm your mind) for at least ten to fifteen minutes. Write down what you want to get rid of and also your affirmations. The order of factors does not change the result, consequently whatever order you choose, the important thing is that you make time for writing.

Write freely, changing hands

After your meditation, sit down with your journal and write freely about what you feel.

The process is easy: you will write your feelings in each working area. How do you feel about writing? Like an adolescent? Are you happy that you are taking action about what does not satisfy you? Write about everything you see and feel. One of the recommendations is to write down what came to your mind while you were meditating. Write down any image, sound, smell or feeling you experienced. For example: if you smell roses, write it down. If you hear any kind of sound or music, write what you heard. Later read your expressions silently and then read them again aloud, without any type of judgment; just meditate about it.

At first write with your dominant hand and then with the non dominant one. When you feel it is enough time, change hands. See what you express when you use your dominant hand and check the difference regarding your non dominant hand. Usually writings with the latter give you information about your spiritual and sensitive side, and the dominant one informs about your assertive and controlling side.

The dialogue

It is a part of the journal that gives you information about your fears and about what you have learned. When one of my clients did this part of the work, she understood that she had a series of believes regarding money, which made it impossible for her to earn the amount she wanted. When she saw it on paper, she used affirmations to put new believes in her subconscious mind. I also recommended to her to see a psychologist to work on her family situations which made it impossible for her to move towards her goals.

You can have a dialogue with anything you want. It can be people who are not on this plane, money, what bothers you, people whom you need to forgive. You can dialogue with your emotions, fears, children, objects, addictions…. with everything you want to bring to the light of your consciousness.

Example of my dialogue with a politician:

Politician: How are you? Is everything ok?

Bhama: How nice for you to ask. The situations happening in my country pose a big challenge and it is necessary to look for viable alternatives to end criminality, poverty and the general discomfort of the people.

Politician: We are working on it.

Bhama: That doesn't seem so, however I have learned to trust people until someone proves the contrary. At this moment you have not shown me that I can believe in what you are doing because I don't see satisfactory results.

Politician: What is satisfactory for you?

Bhama: That there aren't so many deaths, that the drug problem and school desertion and everything else that is destroying the country ends.

Politician: How are you willing to help?

Bhama: Well, I know that a change in our country has to start with each person.

As Gandhi said, we have to be the change we want to see happen. Thank you for reminding me that I can be an agent of change.

In this example you can see that the answer lies always within us. The challenge is to look within ourselves. You can achieve it through meditation and with the help of this instrument. Write down your dialogue and see the result.

Seventh Instrument

AFFIRMATIONS

What is an affirmation? An affirmation is a decree we consciously express about things we want to happen in our life; it is a declaration of what we want to state. It is something you choose to think in order to create new and wonderful results.

In a conference called "I can do it" I heard Louise Hay say that anything you express is an affirmation, if you are aware of it or not. Louise Hay is known as the mother of the self-help movement and has written books that are on the best-selling list. Among them is "You can heal your life", which helped me to change and heal mine.

So, why do you declare that everything is difficult, that life is not easy and that everything is uphill if you can look at life from a happy and fun point of view?

When we have an idea, whatever it might be, we sent a signal to the Universe and it materializes. That is why when we have low energy vibration thoughts (desperation, anger, resentment, vengeance), this energy will have direct consequences in our life. The thoughts lead us to the emotions, and they in turn manifest themselves in feelings and words. Words are very powerful, but the feeling they transmit is even more so. It is the energy that propels and makes our thoughts come true. A good affirmation to change our self-perception would be: "*I accept that I am unique, I love myself the way I am.*" Another one could be: "*I am willing to change whatever is necessary to improve my life."* You always have to make your affirmations in the present tense, because the place of power is the present, and when we accept that we want a change in our lives, there is a change at that same instant, that is our power moment. When we understand and are conscious of the fact that it is enough already, that we are not continuing our present situation and we want to change it, events called synchronization or alignment start happening.

One way of getting rid of the chains that bind us is to replace our thoughts of defeat and frustration with those of power. One affirmation I heard from Louise Hay and which I think will help us to increase our energy vibration is: *"I pardon you and you pardon me, I bless you and you bless me."* When we forgive it is easier to have thoughts of love, and when we bless someone, the high energy vibration of that feeling activates our connection with that superior force of Love, that works creates marvelous events in our life and in the lives of everyone surrounding us. One of my clients told me that she had been making affirmations about having more than enough work, which had not been true because at that moment she did not have any clients, and she was in a very challenging financial situation. However, she continued with her affirmations and months later she had so much work that she thought of hiring someone to help her. We do not necessarily have to believe what we are affirming. Do not worry about believing or not, just repeat the affirmations. It is much better if we believe in it, because we activate the Divine Energy of the Universe, and together with our action plan, we can make what we are declaring come true.

The techniques:

The commitment is to repeat the recommended affirmations every day, 15 times at least for each one, with the help of any of the given methods. Repetition helps you to record them in your subconscious mind, until it believes they are real. If you can repeat them 15 times with each of the recommended methods, it will be much better.

Always make them in the present tense and in a positive way. Instead of saying: *"I want the love of my life"*, you can affirm: *"the love of my life is with me right here and now"*

Keep the affirmations short so you can repeat them like a mantra.

Mantra = Man means "mind" - emotional aspect – and tra "to free" - transcend -, which we could translate as: to free the mind from the chains that bind it. That makes it easier to write, say and chant them.

Methods:

Write them with your dominant and non dominant hand. Put sound to your affirmations, saying them aloud. Put melody and sing them. Dance, make your affirmations to the rhythm of music.

Paint your affirmations, put color to your feelings.

Preserve your affirmations, look for representative images and create a *Scrapbook* of what you are affirming.

Eighth Instrument

VISUALIZATIONS

Visualizing is creating a mental image of what you want to achieve. When we do it, we put emotion into the image and mentally we use the five senses. We see, smell, taste, hear and touch what we want to manifest. When we visualize we are using our imagination to actively create what we dream about: success, abundance, love and health among other things. If we want to be successful in what we started, we can see and imagine that we have reached our desired goals. We see how people congratulate us and we hear their words of support. We feel their hands shaking ours, we can smell the scent of the environment and savor our success. Here we are using our senses. Always visualize that the goal you want to reach is happening here and now. Do it at least twice a day, when you get up and before you go to sleep. When you get up the mind is relaxed and the process of "seeing" what you want to manifest is easier. Before you go to sleep meditate to let go of all the thoughts of the day. That relaxes your mind and you can fill it with all the details of your visualizations.

The Techniques:
The Wheel of Fortune Map

It is a visual instrument in which you will put photos, magazine images, or whatever you think visibly and clearly represents the result of your objectives. It is a map of what you want to manifest. It is frequently called the Treasure Map. You can make it the size you prefer; it can be round, square, octagonal, according to how much you feel it in tune with your energy. Before you start preparing your Wheel of Fortune Map, meditate at least 10 to 15 minutes and then start your master piece with a relaxed mind,, begin to create your future. It is recommended that you review your map according to what you manifested is appearing; that way you can add anything you like because there will be new goals on our way. When your objectives come up, thank the Universe and keep your map for some time. Later you can perform a ritual of detachment and discard it. This ritual can be burning it (with all the necessary precautions) and thank the Universe for everything it has given you. It is an excellent moment to share your blessings. You can also make a "Gratitude" book, with the photos of what you manifested already and gives thanks for it.

Emotions

When you put emotion and feelings in your visualization, you add energy and creative vibration, which help in the manifestation of what you desire. Abraham, a group of very wise and loving Masters, which Esther Hicks describes as *"an ineffable non-physical phenomenon"* which is channeled through her, says that emotions are energy vibrations we have to synchronize with the feeling of what we want to achieve. Through Esther they has written several books that are on the best selling list, among them : *Ask and it is Given* and *The Law of Attraction.* She and her husband Jerry Hicks travel around the world presenting workshops with Abraham's teachings. The Universe and my visualizations (as soon as I read *Ask and it is Given,* I made the petition and the Universe responded) took me to listen to Abraham at the "I can do it" workshops in Orlando in 2006. There Abraham taught us that what we want in this life starts with three *steps:* 1) asking, 2) the Universe (or the Divine Source) answers, 3) synchronizing with the vibration of the manifestation. The Universe is ruled by several laws. One of it is the Law of Attraction. When we want something, we send out vibrations to the Universe and through the Law of Attraction we bring about manifestations of what we desire.

The group describes the Universe as the Source, and they explained to us that it becomes the vibration of what we want to manifest. In order to show how being aligned with the vibration frequency of the Universe works, Abraham makes an allegory between the river and our life. When we go with the current, everything we wish for will manifest itself because the Source sustains us. On the other hand, if we do not go with the current, we bring up negative emotions like discouragement, deception, disillusion, preoccupation, frustration, laments and resistance, giving way to pain and suffering. In order to go with the current it is necessary to observe our emotions, because we always receive an exact match of what we feel. They show us how close or how far we are from what we wish for. The higher the vibrations, the more energy we are generating to reach our goals. The emotions with the highest energy vibrations are: love, compassion, appreciation, joy, confidence in the Universe, gratitude and forgiveness. It is necessary to really understand that we are generating these vibrations all the time and that we are always projecting them towards the future. Vibration is creation, it is the point of attraction, and the higher it is, the more we attract what we want to manifest itself. Always remember that the point of attraction is in the present, it is here and now.

Energy vibrates at different frequencies. It is like looking for your favorite station on your car radio or at home. Before you find it, what you hear is interference until when you "tune in" with the station you can hear the music clearly. That is why they are called "broadcasting stations" because they emit a signal which your receptor (radio) catches. Our body is like this. Our antenna is the spine and our broadcasting station is the brain. When we think of something, we send a signal that is going to "tune in" with what was not manifested in order to bring it to manifestation. We are energy and we are going to attract events and circumstances to our lives which are in tune with our energy vibration, or rather "as within, so without".

Abraham recommends meditation to get relaxed and increase our energy vibration. After meditation think of the situation you want to change and make peace with it. Look for something positive to increase your vibration. For example: if you need more money do not complain, look for emotions that can increase your vibration, appreciate what you have, give thanks for being alive and being able to work for your change. When you are thankful and appreciative, energy vibration will go up little by little. Your attitude will change and you will feel joy because of all the good things that start to happen, which are nothing else but the Fountain manifesting all you asked for through your vibration.

Ready for an adventure? Lie down comfortably and close your eyes. Imagine that you are walking towards your kitchen. Observe everything in it. Look at the color of your appliances and how they are arranged. When you see the refrigerator, walk towards it. Open it and look at everything inside. Among the things inside you will see a lemon; take it. Close the refrigerator and walk to the place of your kitchen utensils. Grab a knife, go to a safe place and cut the lemon in half. Take one half and look at its color and form.

Lift it up to your nose and smell its aroma. Bite into it, feel the juice entering your mouth. Now, put everything back into its place and when you are ready, open your eyes.

Could you feel how your mouth was filling with liquid only by thinking that the lemon is bitter?

To imagine

There are people for whom visualizing is a true challenge; however all of us can imagine. Our mind takes us places we have always dreamed of. In order to imagine you only have to close your eyes and see what you wish for.

When we visualize we put all our senses to it. When we imagine, we use the mind to see within ourselves the final result of what we want to achieve.

Ninth Instrument

ACTION PLAN

While I was writing this book, my editor, the beloved Yoga Sanjeeda (Gizelle Borrero) asked me consistently "What is an action plan?" and she repeated over and over: *"You have to explain it"*.

How do I design my action plan?" For me the process consists of several steps:

1. Meditating
2. Filling in the Mandala for Transformation
3. Practicing Yoga
4. See the message of Tarot
5. Asking: What do I want? (Meditative Coaching)
6. Putting it in writing (Meditative Writing)
7. Affirming that I have it already and giving thanks for it
8. Visualizing what I wish for
9. Taking action (Prepare the Plan)

This book is a good example of what manifestation has been in my life. I never imagined that I could write. However when my teacher Shanti told me that I could do it, I remembered a prize that I had won in elementary school for a story I had written. The memory of that was deeply submerged in my mind, and therefore I had not remembered it until that moment. But immediately the ego activated one of its common limiting messages: *"The fact that I wrote a story when I was seven years old does not turn me into a writer and much less permits me to write a book."* In moments like this we have to transcend negative messages with which the ego bombards us. At a certain moment I heard my Superior Being tell me: *"And what do you have to lose? On the contrary, you can have the marvelous experience it must be to write a book."* It is always convenient to pay attention to our inner dialogue. The main objective we should consider is learning to distinguish the voice of the ego and the voice of our conscience, and this is achieved by MEDITATING and with our spiritual practice. The voice of our Ego is full of fear, the voice of the Higher Self in us is always the voice of love.

When I arrived home I took a delightful bath (water is the ultimate cleanser) and I started meditating about the seed awakened in my mind. Could I write a book? What would its topic be? What would the steps to follow be? Who would help me to publish it? Well, so many questions came up inside me that for a moment I thought that this was not for me. Again the ego made me think that I was not a writer, so I asked myself again: Why and what would I write a book for? At that moment I heard my Superior Being say: "Do it".

Immediately I thought of a series of my writings published in El Nuevo Día which I could collect and publish in a book. LOL (laugh out loud). I did not know what the Universe had prepared for me!!!

That is how I started the nine step process:

1. I meditated deeply.
2. I filled out the Mandala for Transformation, and I saw that in area Num. V, Creativity/ Fun the energy was very low. That was an opportunity to transcend fears and move the wheel. My goal was to increase energy up to 10.
3. I did Hatha-Yoga. I sat in Sukhasana (an easy pose) and continued meditating.
4. I checked the Tarot to see what its message was. The Sun, a positive card, which gives us the message that our goals

and objectives can be reached if we put determination and energy behind the action, came up.

5. I did Meditative Coaching What is it I want? With my journal in my hand, I asked myself the following questions: Do I really want to write a book? Why do I want to do it? "Yes, I want to write it, it is an adventure I want to experience." "I want to do it so it becomes an instrument with which the person who reads it can change his/her life". "I would like to share everything I learned so it could benefit everybody."

6. I did Meditative Writing (The Journal). I wrote everything I wanted to achieve and obtain with the publication of the book. I wrote down my fears and I understood that I had a lot to transcend in order to reach my objective. I wrote and wrote and wrote without thinking about grammar or if it sounded ok or if it was correct or incorrect. I simply did it. When I read what I had written, I noticed that I had let go of many fears. Right now I am still afraid, but the wonderful thing is that I have instruments to release the fear or put it in "parking", and do what I want to do.

7. I affirmed that I had it already (affirmations in the present tense).

    *   This book is an instrument of transformation for everybody who reads it.
    *   I accept that the Universe has a purpose regarding this book and I surrender to the Divine Presence of Light within me.
    *   I appreciate and love this transformation book for myself and everyone who reads it.
        In the affirmations I included my thanks because I already have it.
    *   Thank you Universe for the many blessing you are giving the readers who put the teachings of this book into practice.
    *   Thank you beloved Universe for this beautiful book.

8. I visualized what I desired. In the Savasana (resting) pose, I visualized the final result. What the book looked like, the cover, how many pages it had. Where the presentation would be. I smelled the fresh ink on the paper. I visualized everything I wanted to obtain.

9. I took action (I prepared the Plan). Three weeks after having made the decision, I went to Shanti and told her: "*Teacher, I am ready, I'm going to write the book*". Her answer was: "*Very good, I have the person who can help you*". That is the way all the doors opened so you can read the book at this moment.

I met my editor and wonderful events happened so that this work could come to light. Once you do the small big step (a phrase Yoga Sanjeeda helped me to develop), the Universe starts to put people, circumstances, information and events into your life which help you to achieve your objectives.

What had the Universe prepared for me? A fantastic editor, who through this work became my friend. She always helped me and gave me Meditative Coaching: "*What is this or that thing?*" "*You have to explain it*".

My first appointment with Yoga Sanjeeda (Gizelle Borrero)

We talked a lot, she coached me, and I wrote down what I wanted to achieve with this book. Our initial meetings were revealing for me. I had found a person who fervently believed in the same thing I did. When we exchanged data, I showed her the interviews from the newspapers Primera Hora and El Nuevo Día and all of the articles that I wrote for El Nuevo Dia. Then she told me: "*Your book has to be about the work you are doing with Yoga and Tarot.*" Oh blessed Universe, now you really made it challenging for me! "*I thought that it was very easy to just collect my writings and publish them, but no, You have another plan for me and I accept it.*" I let go of any preconceived notions and surrendered to the new adventure.

45

When we were working on Area Number I (corresponding to Identity) together, Yoga Sanjeeda taught me that it is more difficult for some people to know what they do not want than what they want. At the beginning I wanted to see everything from a positive angle. Nevertheless, the new experience showed me that what she told me is true. If I ask some of my clients what it is they really wish for, some of them do not know how to explain it, and many times their answer is "I don't know." Sometimes this is because they do not know how to make their wish come true. If not knowing what you want is your case, think of what you do not want, and you will get the answer.

However, even if this process can help you to clarify your true desires, it is not advisable, because when you think of what you do not want you could bring it to manifestation due to the Law of Attraction. Consequently, if you really have to do it that way, try to do it for a really short time and change your focus to a positive vision as fast as possible.

Remember, that where you put your focus it increases, for example: if you focus on lack of money, every day you will have more financial challenges; and where you put your attention, there is expansion, that is what happens when you are obsessed with your weight, your body will expand because of this preoccupation.

After having integrated all the recommended steps into Yoga-Tarot for Transformation, I can say that this integrated method works because I have lived it. The only thing is to do it because you believe you are going to obtain what you desire and you have to be sure that it benefits everybody.

Pray with faith, chant your favorite mantras, do your spiritual practice (the one you choose and feel happy doing) and you will see the results.

AREAS OF THE WHEEL

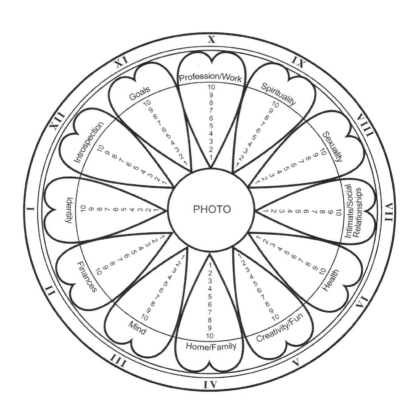

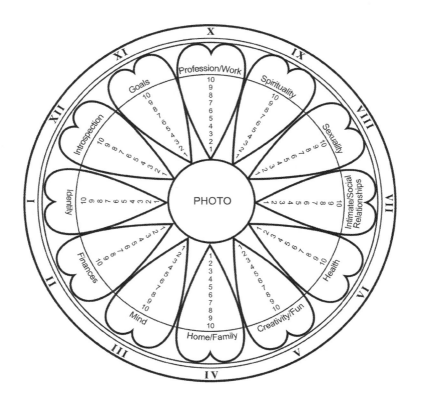

AREA I
IDENTITY

Area 1

IDENTITY

In order to work on all areas of our life, we have to know first who we are and understand our identity. For me an identity is a set of qualities which make us unique and different from everybody else without losing the essence that unites us as spiritual beings. Those qualities are the ones that distinguish us and make it possible for us to stand firm against the maelstrom of the masses. They help us to be observers of events without being affected by them.

When we look for an answer to the eternal question of humanity: Who am I? it forces us to go on an inner journey. I heard someone say once that *"the way is towards the inner self"*. The answer is always within us, but it is a challenge to search within our deepest self, because many times there are situations we do not want to remember. On the other hand, if we want to advance in the process of self-knowledge and self realization, we have to take the "monster" by the horns. Confronting our fear, taking the skeletons out of the closet and analyzing what is happening in our lives is absolutely unavoidable.

One of the definitions that the dictionary of the Royal Spanish Academy offers for identity is *"Consciousness a person has to be himself or herself and being different from the others."* According to some spiritual traditions we are a state of consciousness or a collection of experiences. Other traditions depict us as spiritual beings who have a human experience. The circumstances we live mark our life, and the way we react to the events that happen to us every day makes us different from others.

In this first area, Identity, we are going to work on discovering who we really are. How am I? What moves me to action? What is my temperament? Am I happy and fun or is everything an effort and I see life grey instead of pink? What is my connection with

God or the Universe?

The remaining areas of our life are influenced by the way we see ourselves as people. Thoughts and emotions (psyche) influence our body (soma) and vice versa. They also influence everything that happens and manifests itself in our life. Even if sometimes we see things clearly, most of the time we see them according to what we have lived and what our state of consciousness is and not the way they really are.

The state of consciousness is the knowledge we have about ourselves, our actions and the way we reflect about them. The American journalist and writer Lynn McTaggert says in her book *"The Intention Experiment"* that experiments were made where it is suggested that consciousness is "a substance out of the limits of the body, a highly ordered energy with the capacity to change physical matter." In my meditation process I recognized this energy as an aura or electromagnetic field. When we use this energy wisely, we can change what we call our reality. We are that powerful, we only have to believe in what we are.

In Marcos 9:23 the Bible says "… *all thing are possible to one who believes.*" If you believe in your heart that you deserve to live a life full of joy and happiness, you will live it. Believing is the result of what we think and feel based on our experiences. When we believe something, we take it for granted, we think it is real. Now it is necessary for you to believe that this work you are going to undertake will give you the expected results and that you will achieve all your goals.

The second time I attended the "I can do it" workshops held in Las Vegas (which according to Dr. Deepak Chopra -writer and lecturer- is the most spiritual city in the world, because it does not pretend what it is not), he gave us a series of questions which would help us to know ourselves and find out who we really are. In the Meditative Coaching Section I will share some of them with you, together with other questions which have to be answered honestly, because the answers will help you to see at which point of the Mandala for Transformation you really are.

There are no good or bad answers, they only take you to see where you are in the Identity area and how well you know yourself. Answer them sincerely and take the necessary time to do so. Do not pressure yourself, this is not a competition; it is a process to know yourself better and admit what you want to improve as a person, and what you want to change in your life.

MEDITATION

Take at least 20 minutes for this meditation. Find a quiet place where you can meditate without being bothered (check the recommendation in the meditation section). Keep your journal with you so that after meditation you can write down any image or understanding that comes to mind.

To enter the space of who you are is transcendental, because when you are going to answer the Meditative Coaching questions, your mind is clearer and relaxed.

Lie down or sit comfortably. Turn on your favorite music or simply start your meditation silently. Close your eyes and pay attention to your breathing, inhale deeply and in case any thought distracts you from your breathing pattern, put your attention back to respiration softly and without stress.

When you inhale ask yourself: Who am I? Exhale. Observe your mind. Inhale again and when you exhale ask yourself again: Who am I? Continue inhaling and exhaling, repeating the question: Who am I? Continue asking yourself: Who am I? and continue with your free flowing breathing. Do not answer the question, observe only. When you think that it is the right moment, slowly open your eyes and look for your journal in order to write any or draw any images, words, numbers, colors, sounds and any other element that has come up before you.

Independently of if you decide to do this once a week or daily, it is necessary to comply with yourself and your process. That is how you will get the results faster than you think.

If you feel that you are bored or fall asleep during meditation, it is time to be compassionate with your mind. Do not judge yourself for that. Continue meditating consistently and you will see that eventually you will achieve a quiet and peaceful mind.

Personally it happened to me that I fell asleep and I had the most illuminating dreams at that moment of my life. So if you sleep, take the opportunity to rest. When you wake up, write the dreams down in your journal. Meditate in order to see what they mean to you. There are very good books about the interpretation of dreams, one I worked with and which I recommend is: A Stream of Dreams, by Leon Nacson.

YOGA

The recommended pose for this area is Sukasana (Easy Pose, pag. 264) with anjali mudra (hands in a praying position). If you do not practice Hatha Yoga, sit down comfortably and meditate.

TAROT

Sit comfortably with the cards of the 22 Mayor Arcana. Spread them and pick one, this is the archetype that will help you to work on this area. Look for the meaning of the card in its section (pages

176-256). Take into consideration that any card can have a meaning inherent to the area you are working on.

MEDITATIVE COACHING

After meditation, decide how you want to work with these questions. You can pick two or three and answer them consciously, detailing each answer. You can do this for several days until you answer them all, or you can – as I did – take one day for each of them. Remember that you are the one who allots the time because you are the only one to know your rhythm. If in the meditation process other questions come up, write them down and work on them. In this phase the objective is to know yourself better and how powerful you are.

1. Who am I?
2. What do I like?
3. What is my favorite food? What do I consider fun? What am I passionate about?
4. What motivates me?
5. What inspires me?
6. Whom do I admire? These are the people I want to be when "I grow up."
7. What are my values and how do they influence my decisions?
8. What is my purpose in life? (There can be more than one; do not limit yourself.)
9. What is it I desire?
10. What is the contribution I want to leave to the world?
11. What are my talents?
12. How can I contribute with my talents and serve other human beings and the environment?
13. What are the qualities I look for in a good friend?
14. What is it I want to achieve in life?
15. What is my mission in life? (You can have more than one)

16. What are the things I appreciate most?
17. What is my vision of the future?
18. What are the best qualities I bring to a good relationship?

As you can see, the questions are directed to discover your strengths and stop focusing on your less energetic areas.

Work with each of them, write answers in your journal and move the wheel. Act on what you want to improve.

Remember that these questions are a guide so you can know yourself better. If new ones come up during meditation write them down, answer them and also work on them.

MEDITATIVE WRITING (THE JOURNAL)

You can answer the Meditative Coaching questions and write your affirmations. This can take from one to two hours, but everything depends on you and how deep you want to go in your process. Write down everything that comes to your mind without judging or changing anything. Do it in a spontaneous way and find out what you would like to improve. It is important to think about and analyze your Meditative Coaching answers. I recommend that you take at least seven days for the answers you want to work with on a deeper level.

My free spirit resisted doing this in a methodical way, so I did it little by little, having much patience with myself. Freely, but steadily I learned that the more consistent I am and the more time I invest in myself and in my process the freer I am. For me freedom is my peace of conscience and spirit.

I know that it is a real challenge to look within ourselves, look straight at pain and continue with our daily life. However it has its compensation. While you are coming to know yourself, you will discover little by little that everything is easy, that everything really has a solution. Love sustains you and you trust God because you know that he is always next to you, within you and you in Him.

While working with my clients I learned that we are equal and all different and that, even if we share the same origin, each of us has our own time and space and it is necessary to respect it.

In order to go up one level on the Mandala for Transformation, you can look for one of the answers to the questions and work on it. If you want to elaborate and improve your values, look for the list of the ones you wrote down. In case you want to improve honesty and acting correctly during this week, analyze your actions and ask yourself if you are honoring the value of honesty with yourself and others. Then take the necessary action according to the quality or value you decided to improve.

When Eugenia came to me through the reference of one of my clients, she told me that she felt lonely, frustrated and disoriented. She was exhausted of trying to quiet her inner voice which was telling her that she had to do something to improve the quality of her life. She confessed to me that she did not know what to do and that she was surviving instead of living. At her job as a psychologist she felt that she could not help her clients if she did not help herself first.

Working with the Mandala for Transformation and picking number two in the Identity area she understood that if she did not find her identity, if she did not know who she was, she could not continue working. She could not work or help others, which was what she wanted to do most.

It took her about two weeks to only answer the question "Who am I?" She meditated every day, asking herself "Who am I?" The answer came to her. For her, becoming aware that she was at one with everything surrounding her, was a discovery. She felt that she had to take responsibility for her life and take action. She discovered that the most important moment is now.

We worked around three months with the topic of Identity. She read all the books recommended for this area and she did all her growing work: she meditated 20 minutes in the morning and 20 in the evening. Although she was not a yoga practitioner she did the suggested poses that were modified and adapted to her voluminous body. She wrote down the answers to the questions of Meditative Coaching and analyzed each of her answers in order to share them with me. She did her affirmations and visualizations. She dedicated time to her personal development and improvement. It has been a very challenging process, but right now she already knows what she wants and what the purpose of her life is. She has a professional practice which fulfills and satisfies her, and she is happy to help others. Now, after one year, she is still working on the areas she wants to improve and she always goes back to the Identity area, because that is the basis of life for her.

AFFIRMATIONS

The following affirmations are suggestions, use your intuition and make your own. Remember that they always have to be in the present tense and it is recommended that you write them in your journal at least ten or fifteen times, and if you feel like it chant, dance and repeat your affirmations so they will become your mantras.

- I am love
- I am a Being of Light
- The Divine Energy of the Universe lives in me.
- I am at one with the Universe.
- God is within me and I am within Him.
- I am a state of consciousness.

VISUALIZATION

Visualize that you know perfectly who you are. Visualize that you are a being of light, that the Divine Energy of the Universe lives within you. Visualize a ray of clear light entering your seventh chakra (the crown) and bathe you. This ray enters your whole body, from you head going down and coming out at the feet. Imagine it is cleaning all your wounds and all your limiting believes.

ACTION

Action will help you moving up level by level until, little by little, you reach the goal: getting to know yourself better, know who you are, achieve your goals and live the life of your dreams. This will manifest itself by a round and balanced Mandala for Transformation. Get it and look at the number you picked. What small big step can you take to move up one point?

A small big step could be answering all the questions of Meditative Coaching, study and analyze the answers well, setting your goal at doing it within one week or less.

Recommended reading:

You can heal your Life	Louise Hay
The Dark Side of the Light Chasers	Debbie Ford
The Secret of the Shadow	Debbie Ford
Emotional Intelligence	Daniel Goleman
Practicing the Path	Yangsi Rinpoche
A new earth: Awakening	Eckhart Tolle
To your life's purpose	

Identity

Who am I?

A whisper, a sigh, a voice.

Who am I?

Silence, a caress and pain.

Happiness, love, compassion.

Who am I?

I am everything and nothing.

I am light and darkness.

I am the Universe, I am God.

Who am I?

I am conscience.

I am mind.

I am nothing and everything.

Who am I?

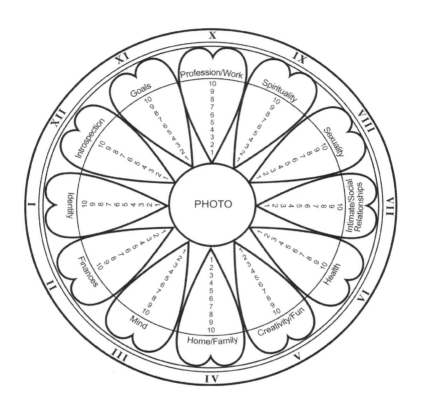

AREA II
FINANCES/MONEY/
PROSPERITY

Area II

FINANCES, MONEY, PROSPERITY

Area II of the Mandala for Transformation is about material possessions. This defines what we have and what we want to have. It represents our main patrimony, spiritual wealth and our purest intentions: to give to others in order to benefit another human being. When we have an altruistic attitude the energy moves in our favor. If we give away something we have – without affecting ourselves – we put Love, the greatest energy, into action. When we love, we can achieve anything because all the blessings the Universe has for us manifest and show themselves.

Area II also represents what we hope to obtain in life, our goals, objectives and our relationship with money.

This area is associated with the second chakra (wheel in Sanskrit), which is the center of our personal power, creativity, sexuality and finances. It is also where Hara is, a term the Japanese use for the center of power, where universal energy is located and stored in the body. According to some schools of thought, there is a central point in Hara, called Tantien which is a very important energy center. In Tai-chi Chuan and in the arts of self defense, all movements originate from that point. When this power center vibrates and pulses rhythmically we can manifest our desires. Yoga and Tai Chi are rhythmic movements which help you to balance the energy of the center.

Practically all aspects of our life are affected by money: work, fun time, creative activities and the family. Everything we do and dream of doing is related to money (one way or another).

Everything is energy and the things we see or do not see are a manifestation of it. There are several representations of energy: money, time, the cell phone we use, everything we look at, the car, the picture we paint, the clothes we put on; in the end everything is energy. Making your dreams and goals come true is using energy positively.

Successful people have learned to focus on and manage these expressions of energy in a way they can manifest what they want. In the book *The Energy of Money,* Maria Nemth (author and clinical psychologist) indicates that Joseph Campbell (speaker, religious historian, philosopher, famous for his studies of religions and comparative mythology) said that *"Money is congealed energy, and releasing it releases life possibilities."* What is a possibility? According to the dictionary of the Royal Spanish Academy it is "ability, power or occasion to do or make something exist: ability and power to do or not to do something." When we liberate the energy of money, we are freeing all our potential to achieve our goals.

When we look at coins and bills we are really looking at a physical manifestation of the energy exchange we live every day. If we want to buy ice cream we need the energy of money. If we need to pay our financial commitments we are using the energy of money to exchange it for goods and services.

How can we liberate this energy? For starters we have to do some inside work to see what our believes are in relation to money. Which of them have been learned and which have been passed on from generation to generation. What did your parents teach you about money? Which of those believes was acquired through your own experience and why do you think that it will always be the same way? Change is the lasting constant, because nothing is forever. Meditate (remember, meditation is the multi medicine) for at least 15 minutes and get your journal. After meditation write your history related to money and let go of limiting believes that keep you from relating with it in a healthy way.

When I had to meditate and reflect about my money history, I remembered something I had forgotten. When I was about seven years old I decided I wanted to start saving in order to open a bank account. I wanted to have money when I was grown up. My aunt gave me the typical piggy bank as a present and it was precious to me. I started saving all the money I was given and I ended up having a considerable amount of money in my piggy bank.

But one day one day we had visitors to our home and mysteriously one morning the piggy bank was broken and the money was gone. I cried disconsolately; it was my first experience of having lost money. I did not understand what had happened, I only knew that something which had cost me a lot of effort had evaporated from one day to another. My mother explained to me later that one of the visitors had an addiction problem. That made them take the money to buy the drugs they needed.

That was my first impression related to money. It probably was recorded in my subconscious mind as: Why make such an effort to keep something that was going to be lost when someone would take it or it would vanish? So, unknowingly the child in me started to spend all the money that came into my hands, buying what she wanted and enjoying what she had acquired. That pattern repeated itself until I became an adult and it took me through a string of debt and credit cards of all kinds and colors. Loans to pay the credit cards and using them again later. A seemingly endless chain. Pain, suffering and the stress of not being able to pay my debt made me sick.

When I started my process with my teacher Shanti I understood that things do not have to happen the same way again. We worked a lot on the abundance area until I recorded something different in my subconscious mind. I made many affirmations and visualizations. I affirmed that *"money is more than enough and it manifests itself in different ways in my life,"* and I visualized all my debts paid. I learned that sometimes money you owe is really a karmic debt. That, as with Karma, if I were diligent and consistent in my joyful effort I would be able to pay them. I understood and absorbed into my conscience that money is energy, it moves, it circulates, it leaves me to help others and then comes back to help me.

When Cassandra came to see me, she had previously had such a painful experience with money that we worked for more than a year on her situation. Her first experience with money was of a sexual nature. When she was eight years old, a neighbor touched her genitals and breasts and then gave her money. At that age she could not realize that that man was abusing her, she only knew that she felt uncomfortable when he touched her but likes the money he gave her because she could buy the things she liked. Nobody ever taught her that letting herself being touched was something incorrect, and her parents did not ask her where she got the money either. This pattern continued until one day the neighbor moved away and she did not see him again. She did not get the money anymore she used to buy toys with, and she was also left with the wrong impression that in order to have money she had to get sexually involved.

She had one relationship after the other, tormented by the thought that she was used only for sexual pleasure. Each partner was an emotional drag for her where she felt that in order to be loved she had to sell herself. Each man in her life represented the act of paying for all her cravings, jewelry, luxuries, and sometimes she felt that she was acting like a prostitute. She wanted to feel loved and she herself wanted to love, but she did not know how to do it.

When she made a mark on number I of the Mandala for Transformation for her sexuality and also for the money area, she understood that she had compromised her identity in order to buy everything she craved. She discovered that she really did not need the objects, it was simply the fact of spending and buying. It was like a drug, she felt the daze and numbness when she was spending, and later she entered the whirlwind of guilt. Over time she realized that she was not so young anymore and that she had no savings.

On an unconscious level she did not want to keep something that had caused her so much pain, because she associated money with what for her was the loss of her innocence and the fact that she had permitted her body to be violated. Now she wanted to do something to make money for her retirement.

After six weeks of doing her recommended pose, meditating, reading, affirming, writing and visualizing she felt that a change had happened. It was nearly imperceptible, but it was strong enough to help her to get out of the vortex that engulfed her. She was able to recognize that she was not guilty of what had happened, and when she did the forgiveness exercises she felt free from the guilt she had carried for so many years. During the process of analysis and answering the questions of the Meditative Coaching, she discovered that honesty was transcendental for getting out of the stagnation she was in.

In one of the meditations she saw that she could look for another way of generating money energy. She started to meditate about it and after a few days she met a childhood friend. In their conversation her friend told Cassandra that she was working in a multilevel company, that she was doing very well, and she would invite her to a meeting if she was interested. That was her small big step to generate money for her retirement. At the same time she was helping others to improve their health – because the company sold health natural products - she was helping herself to generate an income for her resting and wisdom years.

Motivation is vital to generate the energy of money. For me the true purpose of money is serving a greater good: help others. Yes it is good to be prosperous, yes it is good to have a house, a car, to be successful, but it is even better to give in order to benefit others and enrich our life doing so. One thing begets another. Energy moves fast when we honor it and use it wisely.

Integrity is another value or ethical principle that attracts money and abundance in our lives. Make a moral inventory of your relationship with money. Did you ever take anything that did not belong to you however small it was? Did you use resources inappropriately? As an example: making copies (for your own use) in your office without asking permission, or when you make a payment and the cashier gives you excess change back and you do not say anything about it. If in a store they give you more merchandise than you paid for and you do not give it back. Using clothes or merchandise and later return it to the store which gives you a reimbursement. ... Even if for some people these attitudes are immaterial, they describe your integrity. Energy has to be honored and respected, if you use resources inadequately, money energy solidifies and it will be difficult to free it. When you examine your conscience and look directly at what you can improve, energy liberates itself. If you take the corresponding action you can achieve wonderful things.

In order to move this energy, count your blessings. Before going to bed meditate and make of things you have to be grateful for. If it is difficult at the beginning, start with three or four, as for example the fact that you are alive, you have a family, you have something to eat and a place to sleep. Every evening add more items to your list until little by little you see it grow and it will be easier for you to do it. Do this for a week and compare the lists.

During this process of liberating stagnant energy the undisciplined mind is going to bombard you with all the old programs and beliefs. *"I cannot do it, money is not sufficient, this is not working."* Remember the antidote: meditation, affirmations (written and spoken), visualizations (first you have to believe it in order to see it) and action.

MEDITATION

I recommend that you set aside at least 15 to 20 minutes for this meditation. The technique is the same: look for a quiet place, disconnect all telephones, turn on your favorite music and sit or lie down comfortably. Close your eyes and focus on respiration, inhale deeply and if any thought distracts you from your respiratory pattern, softly and without stress turn your attention back to respiration.

When you inhale ask yourself "What does money mean to me?" Exhale. Observe your mind. Inhale again and when you exhale ask yourself again "What does money mean to me?" Inhale and exhale again in turn repeating the question "What does money mean to me?" Continue asking yourself "What does money mean to me?" and continue to breathe evenly. Do not answer the question, observe only. When you think it is the right moment, open your eyes and slowly get your journal so you can write down images, words, numbers, colors, sounds or any other element that has shown itself to you.

In the subconscious mind there is a lot of information that is going to enter your conscious mind. There are limiting fears and believes regarding your relationship with money. It is necessary for you to find out what you remember or what you have learned. Have you heard your parents say that money does not grow on trees and much effort is necessary to earn it?

Possibly you say 'I don't remember". At this moment you have to enter an analysis and reflection space, and if you continue meditating you will see how images will come to your mind, and you will remember what you thought you had forgotten.

YOGA

The recommended pose for this area is The Sphinx. This pose will help you to increase the energy vibration of the second chakra, related to sexuality and money. When you increase this energy vibration you can use the energy to manifest what you wish for. My recommendation is to hold this pose for at least one minute or a minute and a half. Always listening to your body and honor it. If you feel uncomfortable, let go of the pose softly and lie down to rest. See the pose on page 265.

TAROT

Sit down comfortably with the 22 Mayor Arcana cards. Spread them and pick one, this is the archetype that will help you to work on this area. Look for the meaning of the card in the section provided for it (see pages 176-256). Take into consideration that each card can have a meaning inherent to the area you are working on.

MEDITATIVE COACHING

1. How do you see money, as a friend or enemy?
2. Do you think that money is not good for anything?
3. What did you do with the first money you earned or which someone gave you as a present?
4. Did you save it? Did you run to buy something?
5. Did your mother or father use your savings? What did they use them for and how do you feel about it?
6. Have you ever lied regarding money?
7. How generous are you with less fortunate people?
8. Have you lost any money? How did you react to it?
9. What do you use money for?
10. How often do you feel that you are spending money compulsively?
11. What do you feel when you spend unconsciously?
12. How do you see yourself financially within five or ten years from now?
13. How do you administer your savings account and your retirement plan?
14. What would have to happen so you can get the money you want?

MEDITATIVE WRITING (THE JOURNAL)

Write down the images and things you remember which came up during meditation and analyze each one. Observe how these experiences are affecting your relationship with money right now. Answer the questions of Meditative Coaching and write them down in your journal. Remember that you are the one who decides the time you work on each of them.

AFFIRMATIONS

- I have more than enough money to do everything I want.
- Money manifests itself in different ways in my life.
- I am a good administrator of the money I get.
- Abundance manifests itself in my life in different ways.
- I recognize and appreciate the abundance of health, love and money in my life.

Use your intuition and make you own affirmations. They have to be in the present tense and short so you can keep them in mind and in all your body.

VISUALIZATION

Visualize having all you need for yourself and to help others. If you cannot see it, maybe your mind is sending scarcity messages and that you do not deserve abundance in your life. "I am not good enough to have what I want." In this case you have to work on affirmations first. A good affirmation I learned from Louise Hay is "I accept that I deserve the best."

ACTION

Write down your action plan to achieve your goals. How much money you need and what you are going to do to bring it into manifestation? Do you need to get another job? Can you sell something or do a service in your spare time? Meditate about possible alternatives and open a bank account for your specific purpose. Prepare a budget and stick to it. What small big step can you take to move up one level on the Mandala for Transformation scale?

I remember having heard Suze Orman (personal finance expert, author of books on the best seller list) say that a woman who feels safe and confident financially is happier (the same applies to men). It is necessary for you to take action. If you see in your analyzing process that you have to start saving and you mistakenly believe that the money you have is not enough, change your thoughts, prepare a budget and save, even if it is only $5.00 a week. This action makes energy move. Give thanks for the fact that you have $5.00 for saving and the Universe will respond to your action. You will see new sources of income. It is like the multiplication of the loaves of bread. At that moment people asked themselves how Jesus had done it, but they did not doubt the miracle and they knew that everybody had been fed.

Recommended reading:

The Energy of Money	Maria Nemeth, Ph.D.
The Secret	Rhonda Byrne
Ask and it is Given	Esther and Jerry Hicks
The Attractor Factor	Joe Vitale
Women & Money	Suze Orman

Finances, Money, Prosperity

Money is my friend.

It comes to me easily.

It grows on trees.

It blesses everybody with its presence.

It crosses mountains and rivers.

It does not stop.

It multiplies in the presence of

those who honor its intelligence.

It is part of me, and I am part of it.

We are one.

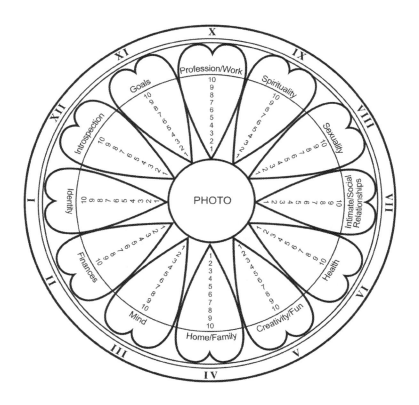

AREA III
MIND

Area III

THE MIND

The word mind comes from Latin mentis, which means: intellectual powers of the soul. In the dictionary of the Royal Spanish Academy it says that in psychological terms it is a "*Set of conscious or unconscious psychic activities and processes specially of cognitive nature.*" More than 2.500 years ago, Shakyamuni Buda said that everything is in the mind. Since then this topic has become one of the most studied and analyzed ones in history. It has been the object of treaties, analyses and controversies. Some people explain that the mind itself does not exist and that everything is a product of brain activity, while others assure that the mind is everything. However up to this moment it continues to be a mystery. Several groups of thinkers affirm that the mind is an archive of memories and experiences. Some spiritual traditions indicate that it is located in the brain and others say that it is in the heart. Apart from that, different scholars claim that the mind is our state of consciousness.

In on-line dictionaries it is pointed out that the mind is a combination of abilities: reasoning, perception, emotion, memory, imagination and will.

In the second Sutra of the book The Yoga Sutras of Patanjali it says that: "Yoga is the cessation of mental fluctuations." When we practice Yoga (Union) the mental buzz ends. We stop identifying with the Me, the Ego, with our body and with what surrounds us, we let go of what keeps us chained to pain and suffering. That moment is called by some people "mind of bright light." When we are in Yoga we achieve the union with our true nature, the light inside us....... that Buddhist and/or Christian nature.

During my trip to India I had the opportunity to attend a conference about meditation by the Venerable Antonio (Tibetan Monk who travels around the world lecturing about Buddhism). He taught us that the mind is like "a wild animal." He advised not to confront it, to simply observe it, look at it with love and compassion until you train it and make it your friend. When we meditate we are in this observation process until we educate our mind and are able to recognize our thoughts. When we explore them, we understand that they cause joy, euphoria, peace, wellbeing, suffering, hate, rage. Sometimes they cause pleasure and sometimes pain.

In a moment of intense and deep pain our mind is so absorbed in the situation or event that it does not let us reason and see all the options that exist to help us to get out of our suffering.

Think of a painful situation you experienced in your life and make an analysis of what you thought and felt at that moment. Observe how your wrong thoughts were the ones that created your feelings and experience. It is always good to remember that thoughts are just that and they deceive us frequently. I have a bumper sticker that reads: "You don't have to believe everything you think." When you are in a situation where your mind tells you it is real, stop, take a deep breath and look for something to do, something to distract you. This will make you gain time to study the situation objectively.

Analyze and consider how it affected the way you acted and how it changed what you said or did. Think of how it upset the people around you.

Do you think that your attitude at that moment was correct? Were you looking at all the angles of the situation or did you only focus on them through your erroneous vision?

What were the consequences of your actions at the moment when you acted with sudden rage ? Analyze, meditate, reflect and think of another way you could have resolved the situation.

What keeps us chained to the cycle of pain and suffering? Tibetan Buddhism teaches us that the deceptions of the mind are at fault. One of the greatest deception is thinking that things or situations are permanent. The attached mind clings to people, things or situations and this sometimes leads to pain, rage, hate and anger (all of them emotions of low vibration frequency). It takes very little time for the mind to distort some circumstance or event. It is important to understand that the mind is like fire, once it starts it is difficult to stop.

Some of the stages we pass through in moments of suffering are rage, anger, attachment (holding on to the situation, person or event) and at the end of the process there is acceptance. Then we understand that sometimes independently from what we do the situation will not change. The things we can change are our way of thinking and our attitude towards what happens to us, but the situation itself does not change. The event itself is neither good nor bad, it is our mind which gives it the characteristics that lead to pain.

According to Tibetan Buddhism each of the stages has an antidote. For the rage and anger stage the antidote is practicing patience, because it is the basis of happiness. When we are patient we have the capacity to examine the situation and not to get upset. When we analyze things objectively we can see all alternatives and angles of a situation.

The antidote to attachment is generosity. It is the wish to give of what we have for the benefit of others. Giving, motivated by bodhicitta (the desire to achieve enlightenment for the benefit of all sentient beings), is the perfection of generosity. When we give with love of what we have to those who need it, we give them support, encouragement, time and service and it gives us a sensation of wellbeing which makes us think that we are giving meaning to our life. A sense of happiness invades us and our joy is evident.

Regular practicing of meditation helps us to understand that happiness is a mental state, it is a state of consciousness and consequently its beginning is in the mind and not in objects outside ourselves. It helps us to cultivate thoughts that create calm, peace and tranquility even in the most adverse circumstances.

Some scientists state that when a thought is in our mind, an electric charge able to light a bulb surges; and others say that the charge could light an entire city. Observe your thoughts, you could ignite a flame, which must always be of love and compassion.

After several months working on this area, Elena lit the flame of love and compassion in her mind. She discovered that when she looked at everybody – including herself - with compassion she saw God in them, life became much easier for her. She had a wrong concept of herself which did not let her see further than what her mind bombarded her with. She told me that there was a chaos of thoughts in her mind which she could not control. She tried to meditate and her mind did not stay "blank." I explained to her that for me to leave the mind "blank" is not meditating. To meditate is to relax, and that was her goal at that moment.

Paying attention to respiration was a big challenge for her. She got frustrated, and even when she tried to do what I had explained to her, she always had an inner dialog at the same time of her meditation. It was as if two people were in her mind. One tried to relax and the other one continued calling her attention to situations and challenges she confronted every day.

In her case, first we worked on Active or Dynamic Meditation by Master Osho (look for the description where The Instruments are explained) so she could let go of her emotions. After that much activity her mind was more relaxed and she could enter the meditation space she was looking for, which is called peace, harmony and serenity. She worked with this technique for around three months and then she did relaxed meditation. When she was doing it she focused on her breathing, and if a thought came up she would softly return her attention to respiration. She practiced relaxed meditation for about four months. This technique helped her to stay alert and be able to recognize her thoughts.

She understood during meditation that she needed to seek help. She had an unhealthy relationship with alcohol. Each time she confronted a challenge in her life, she drank until she was unconscious. She could easily drink one bottle of wine and continue drinking whatever she found to anaesthetize her pain and calm her mind. She also accepted to look for the help of a mental health professional because she suffered from episodes of depression which kept her inactive and only wanting to sleep for days.

Drinking and sleeping were her ways to escape her destructive thoughts. She thought that when she was not accompanied by a man, she was worthless as a woman. If anybody did not agree with her, she concluded that the person did not love her, and she was always looking for approval of others. All this happened at an unconscious level. She had to take power back and put her life on the path she wanted, which simply means being at peace, having a stable couple relationship and being able to develop a new nexus of respect and love with her teenage daughter.

For more than one year we worked on her mental dialogue for which she meditated daily around 20 minutes. She learned to observe her mind and her thoughts. She was able to understand that she did not have to believe everything she was thinking, specially when the things that came to her mind were unfounded. The fact that she failed in her attempt of a romantic relationship did not mean that she was not worth anything and that she was a loser. She understood that many times her thoughts were not real and she could observe how they came and went without getting attached to them.

In our lives events happen that shake us, the important thing is how we react to them. Sometimes we respond with pain, anger or despair. Even though it is important to understand that we can see them as a learning process on this marvelous planet that we call Mother Earth and go our way joyfully because we know that nothing is permanent.

MEDITATION

For this area Relaxed Meditation is recommended (see pages 17-18 for an explanation of the technique). However if there is a buzz in your mind that you cannot stop, do Energetic and Dynamic Meditation first for several days before you start the other one.

Later, when you start Relaxed Meditation, pick one of the questions of Meditative Coaching and reflect about the answers.

Something you can also do is select a mantra (according to the Royal Spanish Academy it consists of holy words or phrases recited to invoke Divinity or as a support in meditation) and repeat it daily. You can choose OM (it is said to be the universal mantra), as your first mantra and chant it daily for at least 15 minutes in the morning and 15 in the evening.

YOGA

The recommended pose for this area is the downward facing dog. Hold it for at least one minute. If you are not a Hatha Yoga practitioner do the pose (see page 266 for an for an explanation). If you cannot do it, sit down comfortably and meditate.

TAROT

Take the cards of the 22 Major Arcana. Spread them and take one, this is the archetype which will help you to work on this area. Look for the meaning of the card in the section provided for it (see pages 176-256). Write in your journal about the meaning this card has for you at this moment.

MEDITATIVE COACHING

1. What previous experience makes me think this way?
2. What can I do in order not to get attached to my false beliefs?

3. How attentive am I when I observe my thoughts?
4. What kind of action do I take when I recognize a low frequency thought (jealousy, rage, rancor)
5. How can I recognize the transience of the events in my life?
6. Are these thoughts real or a product of my imagination?

MEDITATIVE WRITING (THE JOURNAL)

Write experiences, feelings, images, sounds or colors which have entered your mind during the meditation process. Write in your journal your reflections regarding Meditative Writing.

AFFIRMATIONS

- My mind is always alert, attentive and receptive.
- Within me there are only thoughts of peace and harmony.
- My mind is at perfect peace.
- I surrender all my thoughts to God's Divine Intelligence.
- The Divine Light brings clarity to all my thoughts.

VISUALIZATION

Lie down comfortably and put a pillow or cushion under your knees.

Visualize yourself being engulfed in light. Imagine that bright light entering your head. Observe how it cleans all of your brain and gets rid of any attachment. If a color comes up, inhale profoundly. Maintain your visualization for at least 15 minutes. Then open your eyes little by little and look around you attentively. Rest for at least five minutes before getting back to your tasks.

ACTION

What small big step can you take to delve into your mind? One of them could be: every time you think of something that causes anger, pain or despair you look for something to do. For example: dancing, singing, hitting cushions. That is how you give yourself time to change focus. Remember that your are the one who decides which thoughts you want to keep.

Recommended reading:

When Things fall apart — Pema Chödrön
Train Your Mind Change your Brain — Sharon Begley
The Power of Your Subconscious Mind — Dr. Joseph Murphy
Feeling Good — David D. Burns
Molecules of Emotion — Candace B. Pert

The Mind

I am not ME, but you are in me.

I live with you.

I meditate in you.

Mind, sometimes you do not let me live.

But without you…. what would I be without you?

Sometimes I feel

that you are my worst enemy.

But when I can train you

you become

my best friend.

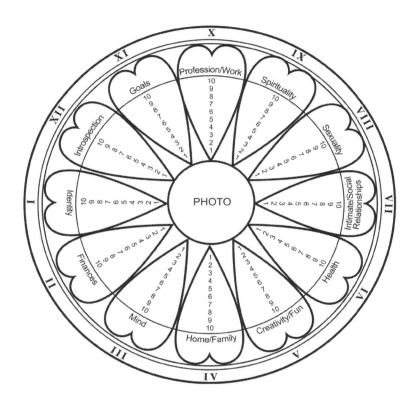

AREA IV
HOME/FAMILY

Area IV

HOME/FAMILY

One of the areas where we possibly have more challenges is with our family. Many times we get the greatest teachings that Divinity has for us in our home. It is with the family and at home where we have been called to practice compassion, patience, equanimity and pardon.

The family is the core of society. The same way we behave with our family members we will behave with our social relationships. It is in our family where we learn and apply the moral and ethical standards that govern our behavior. It is where we learn to say "thank you" and "please", "Can I help you with something?", "What can I do for you?", etc. It is where we learn the difference between right and wrong. Through this family interrelationship we learn to give and receive love, to be compassionate and to forgive. .

Family members play a role formed by society and in this context it is understood that fathers should behave like fathers, mothers like mothers and children like children. There is a hierarchy and specific order where each family member is expected to play his/her role with love. The father is considered the protector and provider, while the mother has the responsibility to give love and strength, and the children are supposed to receive with love what daddy and mommy offer them.

However, close to the end of the XX century and at the beginning of the XXI, the family concept has changed regarding the members. Every day there are more single mothers, and also the amount of single fathers bringing up their children, grandfathers and grandmothers bringing up their grandchildren, uncles and aunts bringing up their nephews and nieces, etc. has increased. That means that a new structural concept has emerged. Moral values of love and support have not changed, only the way how a family is composed.

Now mothers have taken over the father's role and they have to exercise authority and discipline previously expected of him. On the other hand, the single father who dedicated himself to bringing up his children, has had to take over the role of a loving protector when there is no maternal figure present.

All those changes make us reflect on how we want our family to be. Even if we are two people – my daughter or my son and I – we are a family. And …..What is a family? One of the definitions given by the Real Academia Española (Royal Spanish Academy) is *"A group of people who are related to each other and who live together"*. Now there is an increasing number of couples or single people who adopt children, creating a family even if the children are not related by blood.

It is important that you analyze the family concept you personally have and that you share it with your family members. Together you could make a definition about what it means to you and write down its mission and how you can achieve it together.

Even if your family is formed by two people, it is important to remember that the basis for it to be healthy is love, respect and trust. We have to know how to listen, dialogue and negotiate in order to apply those skills when we are at challenging moments. For me, listening actively is one of the most important skills in any relationship and specially in a family one.

When there is a difference of opinion among the parties, we generally cling to our point of view without listening to the one of the other person; without understanding that there are always two faces of the same coin. We want to be right, independently of the consequences. Mostly the disagreement is because we have different points of view regarding the same situation, and one of the parties wants to impose its criteria without taking into consideration the other's opinion.

When we adopt this attitude, there is no possibility of negotiation or understanding because we are stuck with our point of view, and many times we give way to rage. That clouds understanding and does not let us reason. An antidote for rage is being patient, and practicing spirituality will help us to develop it. When we are patient, we can listen to other people. If you feel that you let yourself be dominated by rage - stop, breathe, open your heart to love, observe and listen to the voice of your Superior Being.

Active listening improves communication in the family. Communication begins when we listen. In order to do it in an active way it is necessary to pay attention to the one who speaks, look him/her in the eye, maintain visual contact during the whole conversation and observe body signals. Hearing is only perceiving sounds around us, but listening is much more; it is reflecting about the point of view of the person who speaks and show empathy with the situation. The beginning of peace at home is to know how to listen to, understand and respect the other person.

When we listen actively we pay attention to what is told us, not thinking about what we are going to answer but reflecting about the feelings and concerns of the person who talks to us.

When we listen actively we do not interrupt the person who talks to us, we are immersed in what is being communicated to us. We use expressions that show the person who is talking to us that we are interested in what he/she is telling us.

In order to make sure that we are understanding we have to repeat what we are hearing in our own words. We confirm it with sentences like: I heard that you told me (this or that), Am I right? Did I understand correctly? We validate the feelings of our conversation partners (mother, son, daughter, nephews and nieces, etc.) so that they know that they have every right to feel what they are feeling.

We say sentences like: "It is natural that you feel like this", "It's ok.", "It's normal".

This process makes the person feel save, shows respect from our side, expresses that we are attentive and that we understand what we are being told. This way we develop mutual respect and we understand that our children, mothers, fathers, uncles and siblings have important opinions necessary to be considered. We learn to appreciate all ideas, not only ours but those of others too. That is how we can understand the causes and conditions that led to the disagreement.

If we remain inflexible regarding our point of view, we are denying ourselves love and compassion. When we love we have a genuine interest in the wellbeing of the other person and we can admit that he/she can be right. This gives us the flexibility to change our point of view without feeling that we are "losing" because it is not important to win or lose but to love.

The Dalai Lama (Tibetan spiritual leader and 1989 Nobel Peace Prize winner) says in his book *The Compassionate Life* that true compassion is not based on our projections or expectations but on the needs of other people. How can we know what another person needs? It can be achieved by active listening.

One of my clients – whom I am going to call Beatriz – told me during our Yoga-Tarot for Transformation sessions : *"My daughter does whatever she wants and she does not do what I tell her, she is never with me and she does not listen to me. She is always with her girlfriends and she leaves me alone."* Beatriz was so absorbed in finding a partner that she did not realize that she was losing her daughter's respect and admiration. Her obsession with finding "the love of her life" had taken her to a point where she did not pay attention to anything but looking for a boyfriend and later get married, without paying attention to what her daughter thought or felt. She left her alone many evenings during the week and her teenage daughter took advantage of it going out with her girlfriends and coming home at dawn. The situation had gotten out of her hands and she could not "control" her daughter. After answering the questions of Meditative Coaching she came to the conclusion that she had to get closer to her daughter and listen to what she had to say. There were many unspoken words and unexpressed feeling between them.

When I asked her about the reason her daughter acted this way she answered: *"I have to listen to her and understand why she acts this way"*. Beatriz knew unconsciously that she had not given her daughter quality time, even less listened to her, but she did not want to admit it. Doing so meant to admit that she had failed as a mother. However I explained to her in one of our sessions that my first psychologist told me: *"Nobody is given a child to practice with, our parents do the best they can within their capacities and knowledge.'* In this case the best thing would have been to forgive each other and start a healthy relationship with her daughter.

Debbie Ford, American writer and motivational speaker explains in her book *The Dark Side of the Light Chasers* that we are mirrors and that we attract to our life what we have to learn. What we see in other people really is what we see in ourselves, and when someone's behavior affects us it is because that person has a quality that we have not been able to accept in ourselves. In my client's case both people reflected what they felt and what they thought about the other. Her daughter thought that her mother did not love her and Beatriz thought it was her daughter who did not love her. Beatriz discovered that she did not love herself and that was why she projected her lack of love onto her daughter. Her daughter had not learned to value, love and respect herself because she had never been exposed to these feelings due to her parents' divorce which had affected her profoundly.

Her mother/daughter relationship improving Action Plan started with an open and sincere dialogue where Beatrice practiced all she had learned in our sessions. She listened actively, she made an activity list together with her daughter where they would be doing things together, only the two of them, and they also strengthened their relationship building efforts with a visit to a trusted psychologist. In less than a year communication between them had improved so much that now they feel that they are in the best relationship of their lives: the one between mother/daughter.

Meditation

Set aside at least 20 minutes for this meditation. Make sure not to be interrupted. Look for a quiet place and disconnect the telephones. Put some soft music on that helps you to relax. Lie down, direct your attention first towards your feet to relax them. Then go up slowly: legs, thighs, arms, torso, neck, face up to the head. Just let go, imagine that all your concerns get out of your head. Pay attention to your inhalation and if a thought comes up, softly focus on breathing again. After 20 minutes open your eyes slowly and breathe. You are in the "here and now".

YOGA

The recommended pose for this area is the Flying Bird. You find the explanation on page

TAROT

Sit down with the 22 Major Arcana cards. Spread them and pick one out, this is the archetype which will help you to work on this area. Look for the meaning of the card in the section provided for it (see pages). Write in your journal the meaning that this card has for you at this moment.

MEDITATIVE COACHING

1. How satisfactory is the relationship I have with each member of my family? Here you can use the Mandala for Transformation (look for the model on page 20 and make a

copy for each family member. Put the name of the person in question in the Family area and make a mar on how satisfied you are with the relationship you have with him/her - with number 1 the least satisfactory number and 10 the most).

2. How satisfied am I with my performance as a mother/father/ tutor,uncle,aunt, etc?
3. How do I feel regarding my responsibilities as a daughter (mother/father)?
4. How do I practice discipline with my children? With love, fear, resentment, rage?
5. How satisfied are my children with our relationship?
6. What is the mission/vision of our family? How well are we complying with it?
7. How many times a week do I make some time to talk to my child?
   How long are the conversations: one hour, half an hour, 15 minutes?
8. How many times do I go out to have fun with my children ?
9. How do I include the spiritual aspect in our family relationship?
10. How much confidence do my children have in me?
11. How is my relationship with my partner and how can I improve it?
12. How many times a month do I spend time alone with my partner?

MEDITATIVE WRITING (THE JOURNAL)

Note in your journal any image, sound, color or sensation that you experienced during meditation. If you have received some information or you have understood or received the answer to one of your worries, write it down in your journal and reflect about it. Also write down the answers to the questions of Meditative Coaching and analyze each one. You decide the time you dedicate to this process and you can answer one or more of the questions. It is your decision.

AFFIRMATIONS

- *I have a happy and healthy family.*
- *My family is united and at peace, we all live harmoniously together.*
- *All my family members honor each other and they respect their differences.*
- *My family is prosperous and lives in the harmony and peace of the Universe.*
- *God is always present in my family.*

VISUALIZATION

Lie down comfortably and make sure that you will not be interrupted. Close your eyes and visualize your whole family united and loving. Visualize everything you want to happen in the family circle. When you finish open your eyes and give thanks as if all your wishes had already been fulfilled.

ACTION

Answer the Meditative Coaching questions and make an Action Plan to move up one level on the Mandala for Transformation. How about a family outing this week? Another activity you could do is buying a board game (if you do not have any) and make time to play with your children. You can also go to fly kites with your children or go bowling. Play, it is one of the best ways to connect with your family.

Recommended reading:

7 Habits of highly effective Families	Stephen H. Covey
Growing up with Values	Maria Elena López and Daniel Violi
100 Simple Secrets of Happy Families	David Niven, PHD
When the Monster awakens	María Antonieta Collins

Home/ Family

My home is the home of light and peace.

My family lives in it,

a united and happy family.

A prosperous and healthy family

that honors the Divinity within

all of us.

My family is the Universal family

of Loving Kindness.

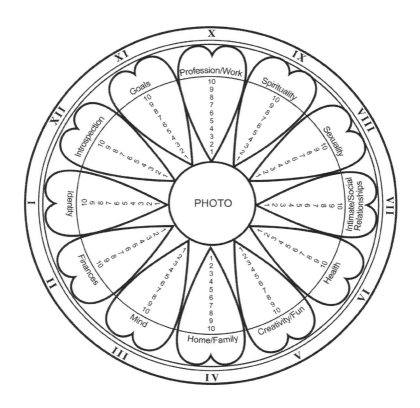

AREA V
CREATIVITY/FUN

Area V

CREATIVITY/FUN

At moments of a financial crisis we generally tend to cut spending on what we wrongly call superfluous, like going to the movies, to a restaurant for dinner, bowling, take a walk with the family among other fun things to do. We believe that by doing this we save money for other "more important things." However it is necessary to have fun exactly at those moments. It has been proven that laughter has therapeutic power which helps us to endure and overcome financial, emotional and physical crises.

Scientific studies demonstrated that laughter lowers arterial pressure, reduces stress, strengthens the immunological system, increases the release of endorphins (small proteins – also called happiness hormones – which reduce physical pain) and make us feel happy.

When we cut off the source of these high energy vibrations like laughter and fun, we are cutting off our creativity. Everything in our life seems to go from bad to worse and events start to happen suddenly that take us out of our comfort zone. We ask ourselves what is happening, without even noticing that we are not having enough fun, and we do not relate negative events in our lives with a lack of fun and creativity.

Many people think that they are not creative. So they cannot notice the relation between creativity and fun. That is why it is necessary for you to ask yourself what creativity means to you. When God created the world – according to theistic religions – he created it out of nowhere. On the other hand some scientists propose the Big Bang theory: that the Universe was created by a huge explosion. Other scientists say that it started expanding and is still doing so. Up to this moment some schools of thoughts believed that the Universe was created out of emptiness, so we could say that being creative is producing something out of nowhere. That means that all of us are creative because at some moment in our life we have had to create something that way.

In order to be creative it is necessary to nourish our inner child, playing and having fun. When we use our creativity, our spiritual practice and meditation we can resolve very challenging situations. If we think that there is no way out of a situation that takes us out of our comfort zone, it is recommended to meditate. When we do it, creative ideas come to our mind that help us to get out of the one way street which we believe to be in. With these ideas we can solve the situation or conflict, making it possible for everyone to win and take advantage of it.

German scientist Albert Einstein said that "we cannot resolve problems by using the same way of thinking we used when we created them." That is why it is necessary to analyze the situation from various angles and use our creativity to think in a different way. Apart from seeing the positive side of situations and what we must learn from them, it is also necessary to find their humoristic side. Once I heard that God has a good sense of humor and that in some situations (which we believe are serious) we always can see something positive. If we let go of attachment and drama, we will see that maybe if we adopt an optimistic attitude we can find something to laugh in the challenge we are living at the moment.

One of the questions I heard from several of my clients is : How can I find something to have fun after I suffered a loss? One of the most painful losses a mother or a father can have is that of a child. Even though, if they think creatively they can understand that children do not belong to us, and this change of attitude makes it possible to accept with love that – from a Christian point of view – God has a purpose for everything and that this son or daughter is already at their place of origin; he or she is already with God, happy and in good spirit. You can find relief from your pain if you think that way. If you use your creative vision you can see your son or daughter in a beautiful garden, laughing and playing with all the angels surrounding them, you can see that they are having fun and you share their enjoyment.

It is recommended that after a loss you take some time to cry, release and let go. Crying constructively is healing and frees us from suffering. However it is important that you watch for signs of depression: unbearable tiredness, persistant sleepiness and a constant desire to cry, little concentration, discouragement, apathy and anxiety among others. If you have any of these signals, it is absolutely necessary that you look for the help of a mental health professional immediately.

About two years ago Bruce came to me recommended by one of my clients. When he filled in the Mandala for Transformation he saw that his energy was on hold at Area number V which corresponds to Fun/Creativity, as well as in Area number IV, corresponding to Home/Family. It was very difficult for him to have fun. That is why his creativity was practically at zero. He needed creative ideas for his job to sell services and products. He had had many challenges in his life lately with the family, work and his relationships. He felt that he was on a dead end. His wife wanted a change in their relationship; she was no longer willing to live "alone" and his children also claimed his presence. Due to the long hours he spent on the job he had neglected his own and his family's life.

When he answered the Meditative Coaching questions, he understood that he felt guilty when he had fun because he thought that he was wasting his time and that it was not productive. His life had become a constant "doing", instead of "being" present for himself and for his family. He had his priorities wrong because he thought that he had to be a good provider which would make him a good father, without noticing that his children preferred to stay with him than go to the movies alone.

He made an action plan of different steps. His family was his priority, so he decided to spend more time with them. In order to be able to do so he got up earlier than he used to, to have breakfast with them. He chose to take them to school twice a week and on weekends they planned different activities together. If he had to work he would take his work home and make time for it there. This seemed more convenient to him, because if he went to the office he would end up working all day. He felt that at home he could control time better and he was close to his children. He even included them in his work many times, asking them for ideas and suggestions.

For me this plan seemed very simple, but for Bruce it was a real challenge working with the guilt feeling he had because he could not fulfill every whim- even unnecessary ones - his children had. In the course of time he understood that for them the most precious gift was his presence and to have fun together with him.

For his creativity issue on hold, he read all the recommended publications and worked with Julia Cameron's book *The Artist's Way,* one of the first books that Shanti recommended to me during my conscious recovery process. Every morning he got up to meditate, do the Morning Pages (an exercise recommended by Cameron in her book) and then he had breakfast with his family. That meant that on the days he had to take the children to school he would get up at 4:30 in the morning. At the beginning it was a true sacrifice, but now he sees it as a "joyous effort" to achieve the harmony, peace and happiness he is living with his family. At the same time this increased his creativity which made it possible for him to be more successful in his job and getting a salary increase and an assistant. That shows that when we do the right thing – as Paulo Coelho says in *The Alchemist* – "the entire Universe conspires in our favor ".

MEDITATION

For this meditation set aside at least 20 minutes in your agenda. Make sure that nobody interrupts you. Look for a quiet place and disconnect the telephones. You can turn on soft music that helps you to relax. Put your attention on your inhalation and if a thought comes up, softly put your attention back on your breathing. Practice Laughter Meditation. My teacher Shanti taught me, and she in turn had learned it from Spiritual Master Osho. Start laughing uncontrollably; at the beginning you might feel a little strange but after some time you will notice that you cannot control your laughter. Remember that when you laugh the brain releases endorphins that help you to improve your mind and body functions. At the end of the time you separate for this meditation, breath in profoundly and write your experiences in your journal.

YOGA

The recommended pose for this area is the Happy Baby. Even if this is a simple pose, if you have any difficulty doing it, practice the adapted pose shown on page 268.

TAROT

Take the 22 Major Arcana cards. Choose one of the recommended spreads and observe which card the Tarot shows you. This is the archetype which will help you to work on this area. Look for the meaning of the card in the section provided for it (see pages 176-256). After looking for the definition write in your journal the meaning that this card has for you at this moment.

MEDITATIVE COACHING

1. What do I like to do for fun?
2. What makes me feel joyful?
3. What makes me feel creative?
4. When was the last time I created something?
5. What has to happen so that I can make time and create something I like?
6. Which activities that I consider fun do I include in my daily life?
7. What is my favorite place and how many times do I visit it?
8. What is my daily schedule to have fun?
9. How guilty or bothered do I feel when I have fun? Why is that the case?
10. What voice from the past tells me that I cannot have fun?
11. What images come to my mind and how do I feel?
12. What keeps me from having fun?
13. How many vacation days do I take in a year?
14. How do I plan my vacations?
15. What would have to happen for me to have fun without feeling guilty?
16. Which activities would I have to include in my daily routine to move up one level on the Mandala for Transformation?

MEDITATIVE WRITING (THE JOURNAL)

Write in your journal any image, sound, color or sensation you experienced during meditation.

Write down the answers to the Meditative Coaching questions and reflect about each of them. Use the techniques recommended by Julia Cameron in "The Artist's Way": write the three morning pages for 21 days, that will help you to increase your creativity. This technique consists of writing the three pages every morning, for at least fifteen minutes. Just write, putting on the paper everything that comes out of your mind.

AFFIRMATIONS

- Having fun is a good thing, I accept that when I have fun I honor the Divinity within me.
- I forgive myself for feeling guilty when I am having fun.
- I give thanks for being a channel for Divine creativity.
- Creativity flows easily within me.
- Divine Intelligence flows through me with great ideas.
- I see my creation with eyes of love.
- I am willing to change the patterns that make me feel guilty when I am having fun.
- I am filled with love, creativity and joy.

VISUALIZATION

Lie down comfortably and make sure that nobody interrupts you. Close you eyes and visualize yourself having fun and doing what you like most and what makes you laugh. Imagine that you are at your favorite place and enjoy it. When you finish your visualization pick up your calendar and make an appointment with yourself to do what you love so much.

ACTION

What small big step can you take to have fun; to be creative? This week make some time for it. Go bowling, to the beach, to the river, to the movies, to a museum. Feed your inner child and play with your children, nephews, nieces and grandchildren. Enjoy the energy of youth. Dedicate some time exclusively to yourself (something that Cameron calls "the Artist's Date"), and in case you have a family, make some extra time apart from yours to spend with them. Make a list of your achievements and of the moments you felt creativity skin deep. Repeat what worked for you before and relax.

The fastest way to relax is using our breathing. When you are at a very challenging moment take a walk and breathe deeply, the brain releases endorphins for your wellbeing.

Make time for playing, having fun, take a walk on the beach and then meditate for at least 20 minutes. Allow yourself to activate love, compassion and the good sense of humor in you. You will see your creativity increasing and allowing you to live a life you always dreamt about.

Recommended reading:

Take Time for Your Life	Cheryl Richardson
Life is short, wear your party pants	Loretta LaRoche
The Artist's Way	Julia Cameron
Creative Visualization	Shakti Garwain

Creativity/Fun

When I am having fun I am creative.

I feel that I am creating

when I dance, when I write,

when I sing.

I have fun looking at a flower, a river

and jumping.

When I have fun and

exercise my creativity,

I feel connected with Divinity.

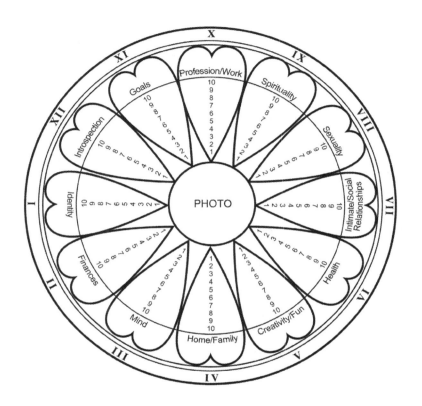

AREA VI
HEALTH

Area VI

HEALTH

If you ask several people what they understand by "health" it is possible that most of them say "not feeling any pain", "not to be sick", "feel physically healthy". That is generally what most people know about health. However what happens with emotional, mental and spiritual health? Is it possible that we think that health does not exist separated from the physical body? We see it sometimes from the perspective of our body, but health also includes the emotional, physical, spiritual and mental aspect. If one of these areas is affected, the others will be too.

I have seen very healthy overweight people who do not suffer from any weight-related illnesses. I have also worked with people who seem to be in a good physical shape who had high pressure, diabetes, high cholesterol and a lot of stress.

American writer and journalist Norman Cousins says in his book *"Anatomy of an Illness"* that we are responsible for our health and that we have to take control of our healing process. While he was suffering from an illness that inhibited movement he discovered that loud laughter for at least ten minutes a day had an anesthetic effect that allowed him to get two hours of restful sleep and made his pain go away. He decided to follow his own treatment and his family doctor helped him in the process. He rented movies that made him laugh, he started a Vitamin C treatment and other unconventional therapeutic processes. He discovered that his ardent desire to live had helped him to recover, and a little later he decided to write the book so it could be of help to others who like him want to take control of their healing process.

Studies were conducted in several universities and laboratories around the world about the body-mind connection, proving that an attitude that is positive, joyful and which believes in the healing wisdom of the body, is vital for the prevention of diseases. So much so that prestigious universities in the United States and in other parts of the world offer body-mind connected courses in their continuing education curriculum.

In order to get information about this topic, I attended Continuing Education Workshops/Talks of the prestigious Harvard University Medical School. Dr. Christina Puchalski, founder and director of the George Washington Institute for Spirituality and Health (GWish) offered us a talk about the subject of spirituality and its importance in the healing of patients.

In order to integrate spirituality and healing it is necessary to know how these concepts are defined. As I understood Dr. Puchalski definition of spirituality as: "spirituality is that part of our being that longs to find a sense of purpose in life; to know that it has a purpose; to experience hope amidst chaos and desolation; to seek pardon and freedom. It can be expressed in philosophical and religious terms or personal believes which integrate values and ethics codes into a person's behavior. Spirituality is that part of a human being that tries to understand who we are in this vast Universe and what our purpose in life is." On the other hand healing is "something more than a disease in remission. It is re-establishing the sense of balance, purpose of life, unification with what surrounds us and a positive relationship with oneself, with others and with God."

During the talks other people versed in this subject explained that apart from a treatment by a health care professional, there are three components that help in the healing process: pardon, hope and compassion. The other lecturers presented studies showing that when we practice one of the three components our well-being increases and the body responds positively because the energy generated by any of them helps us to work on the challenge we are facing.

Our attitude towards life and towards the disease we are confronting is vital for the body to heal. If we take a defeatist attitude, the mind signals to the body that we are very low on energy and the body will act according to this feeling. Many studies had demonstrated the connection between mind and body. It has been seen for example, that Yoga helped carpal tunnel syndrome patients. It has also been proven that when a person meditates and is willing to forgive, anxiety levels go down which lowers arterial pressure. Depression is also controlled and heart attack incidents are reduced.

When we go through a disease process, be it ours or that of a loved one, we generally hope that we get out of the situation we are in. According to studies, hope is effective to help us during a loss. Hoping that the person will be at a better place helps us to endure suffering and the uncertainty of not knowing the final result of the situation we are going through at the moment.

Studies have also shown that cultivating spirituality can help people to endure the difficult moments they will face during their healing process. It is also associated with an improvement in patients' quality of life, it has positive effects on the immunological system and helps to manage the pain of a disease better.

On the other hand, when we show a compassionate and loving attitude towards sick people and ourselves, positive results come up which reduce the symptoms of depression and stress caused by lack of vitality in our body-mind.

The highly regarded human body is the vehicle with which we interact physically. That is why it is necessary to make sure that our instrument is tuned and in the best possible condition. The ways we can refine it are: meditation, prayer, a healthy nutrition based on pure food and exercise like: walking, practicing Yoga, Tai Chi or Chi Kung. That is how we make sure that this body which is "a spiritual temple" for the Divine expression of Love (the Temple of the

105

Holy Spirit for Christians) is in the best condition. When the body is at its maximum potential we have a great consciousness within, we participate actively in our evolution process as well as in the true progress of our planetary brothers.

The body is a power plant that uses the backbone, the nervous system and the chakras as antennas. The electricity to operate the plant is Energy, Chi or Prana and the contents of the energy we emit are our thoughts, emotions and our state of mind.

Gregg Braden (writer, lecturer and scientist) tells us in an I can do it Conference, that emotions are energy in movement and that thought + emotion = feelings. We could say that feelings are the result of vibration emitted by brain energy and that we can tune into our energy vibration frequency by focusing specifically on our conscience.

According to several studies there are two emotions from which feelings originate: love and fear. The feeling of fear which is of low energy, gives way to feelings like fury, hate, dependency, indifference, rage, anger, sadness, depression and envy, among others. They could make mind and body sick. On the other hand, the emotion of love creates sentiments like compassion, joy, peace, serenity, pleasure, admiration, etc. These feelings help us to maintain a high energy level and make it possible for mind and body to be in optimal conditions.

Our body is equipped with seven main energy centers called chakras. Each chakra (or wheel) emanates energy to work with different situations. Caroline Myss, writer and inspirer, who uses her intuition to find emotional causes in diseases, tells us in her book *Anatomy of the Spirit* that the first chakra is the basic energy center and has to do with family, livelihood, the tribe. The organs related to this chakra are: the base of the spine, the immunological system, bones, feet and the rectum.

Other authors also coincide with her that the second chakra is the center of personal power, creativity, sexuality and finances. The organs are: the large intestine, the sexual organs, the pelvis, the hips and the bladder. The third one helps us to develop our self-esteem and personality. The related organs are: stomach, liver and pancreas. This chakra is known as the solar plexus. The fourth chakra (Chakra of the Heart) is the center of the body's energy system. The heart emanates the highest frequency vibration of the human body and the related organs are: the heart, lungs, the diaphragm and the thymus gland.

The fifth one is the challenge of decision-making we have and it also represents communication. The organs influenced by this chakra are: the tonsils, the thyroid, teeth, the neck and the esophagus. The sixth chakra or the Third Eye is the center of intuition, intellect and reasoning. The organs related to this energy center are: eyes, ears, the nose, the pineal gland and the pituitary. The seventh one is the connection to the Divine, it is our spirituality. The organs that respond to its energy are: the skin, the muscular- and the skeletal systems. When the chakras are congested (energy is on hold), the experts say that diseases can happen in the physical body.

What can we do to energize our body? The most recommended actions are: be careful with what we eat, do exercises – specially yoga, Tai-Chi y Chi Kung – which increase the energy of the physical and energetic body. We can also use chromotherapy, music therapy and aromatherapy because for each chakra there is a color, a sound and a smell that activates them.

Additionally, Louise Hay explains in her book *"You can heal your Life"* the different body parts and their meaning. For example: the head is what we show to the world, when it hurts we have to ask ourselves when and how we did not honor our values? The ears represent the capacity to hear and if they hurt, it is necessary to ask ourselves: what is it I don't want to hear? The eyes represent our ability to see. If we get an infection it is convenient to ask: what is it we don't want to see? When our neck hurts, we can analyze it asking ourselves: what is happening in my life that I cannot harmonize reasoning with the heart? The lungs represent the ability to receive and to give, and if they are not in optimal conditions, it is possible that we do not feel that we deserve the best life has to offer. The heart represents love and joy, our blood. When it hurts and our blood does not flow well, we usually have not recognized the little joys that life gives us and we enter so deeply into our situations that we make a drama out of them when it is not necessary. The stomach digests our food, it is the place of our third chakra, the one of emotions. When we have stomach acidity problems it can mean that we have not digested a new experience yet and we are afraid. The colon represents our ability to let go, if you are constipated it is good to ask yourself what is it I don't want to let go of?

Our body is an instrument and we have the responsibility to take care of it and to honor it. Because of it, we have the capacity to live, love and be happy. It is worth taking care of.

MEDITATION

In order for you to enter into deep meditation, set aside at least 20 to 30 minutes for it. The proceedings are the same: disconnect all telephones and make sure that nobody interrupts you. If you like, put soft music on and lie down in the Savasana pose (lie on your back with arms and legs extended). Close your eyes, breathe deeply and focus on your feet. Feel them, observe if you have any sensation: if it is one of wellbeing, continue and focus on your legs. Observe the sensation it gives you, if it is one of relief or if you feel any heaviness in them. Continue going up on your body until you reach your head. You are "scanning" your body to see if the energy is on hold at some place. If you feel that the energy is on hold (it feels like something very heavy at that part of the body), proceed to visualize that a white light enters your head and direct it to the part that needs energy in movement. When the time is up, open your eyes slowly and relax. Write in your journal about what you felt.

YOGA

The recommended pose for this area is the relaxed one, Savasana. Look for the instructions on page 269.

TAROT

Take the 22 Major Arcana cards. Select one of the recommended spreads and observe which card the Tarot shows you, because it is the archetype that will help you to work this area. Look for the meaning of the card in the section provided for it (see pages 176-256). After having looked it up, write down in your journal what this card means to you at this moment.

MEDITATIVE COACHING

1. What is my energy like?
   a. High   b. Low   c. On hold
2. In what part of my body have I felt heat, cold, tingling?
3. What has stopped me from seeing a health professional?
4. What experiences have marked my body and/or mind?
5. What has to happen for me to overcome this situation which is affecting my health?
6. What prevents me from recognizing that I need help?
7. Which fears do tie me down and prevent me from looking for help?
8. How have I grown with this situation?
9. What has been the lesson?
10. What would be the positive consequences of taking any immediate action?

MEDITATIVE WRITING (THE JOURNAL)

Write in your journal any image, sound, color or feeling that you experienced during meditation.

Answer the Meditative Coaching questions and make a mark on the answers that you understand need immediate action.

AFFIRMATIONS

- *I am strong and healthy*
- *My body is beautiful, I love and accept it as it is.*
- *The wisdom of the Universe is within me and I honor the wisdom that my body has to heal.*
- *The Universal Intelligence guides me and I have the capability to listen and act on what my intuition tells me.*
- *I am healthy and I thank God in his infinite mercy for the health I am enjoying.*

VISUALIZATION

Lie down comfortably in Savasana (page 269) and make sure not to be interrupted. Close your eyes, visualize yourself with a strong and healthy body. Imagine creating your body and give light to the parts you want to heal.

ACTION

If you want to improve your health, what small big step can you take? Maybe join a group where Yoga, Tai-Chi or Chi-Kung is practiced. Evaluate the alternatives you have available and act today.

Recommended reading:

You can heal your Life — Louise Hay
Anatomy of the Spirit — Caroline Myss
Anatomy of an Illness — Norman Cousins
Timeless Healing — Dr. Herbert Benson
Mind your Heart — Aggie Casey & Herbert Benson
Perfect Health — Dr. Deepak Chopra
Mueve las ruedas de tu vida — Lily Garcia
Unlocking the Mysteries
of Birth and Death — Daisaku Ikeda

Health

How do I feel today?

In Victory.

How is my body?

Healthy, agile and light.

What is health?

A state of consciousness.

Everything is in my mind.

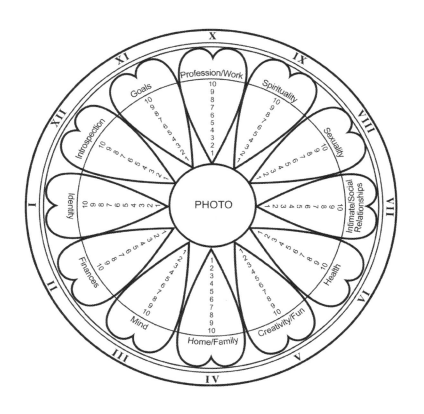

AREA VII
INTIMATE/SOCIAL
RELATIONSHIPS

Area VII

INTIMATE/ SOCIAL RELATIONSHIPS

A relationship is a connection you have with someone. It can be with a person or even with a pet. Relationships can exist for a couple, family or at work. We live in a society and we are constantly relating to each other. We connect with the people who come into our life in different ways, and while the relationship lasts we can convert it into an experience of love and support or one of many challenges.

All events in life are intimately connected to other people. In our family, workplace and around us we are always interacting with someone. That is the reason we laugh, cry, have the opportunity to work, have fun, love and also have experiences of pain, suffering, joy and pleasure.

The most wonderful relationships are the ones that fill us with peace, joy and improve our quality of life, helping us to be better human beings. In order for these relationships with our partner, family, friends, co-workers and the companions of our spiritual journey to be healthy, it is necessary to give and receive love. One relationship that fills us with joy is one of understanding, compassion, acceptance, sincerity, integrity and where we respect each other mutually. Pause for a moment and analyze. Observe if you surround yourself with people who have these qualities. Remember that *as on the inside it is on the outside* and if you want to know how your life is, how you relate to other people, just look around you and observe what you are manifesting.

Human nature is one of love, and we all need to feel loved in order to live. No material object can make us feel love; what our nature requires is something more profound. The spiritual leader from Tibet and winner of the 1989 Nobel Peace Prize, his holiness the Dalai Lama, refers to that "something" as "human affection" in his book *"The Compassionate Life."* We all need affection and compassionate love of another human beings in order to be happy. Nobody, not even the most competent person, can survive without love. We can see a demonstration of this in the movie Cast Away whose main character Chuck Noland (played by actor Tom Hanks) put all his emotions in Wilson (a volleyball) during the time he was on the island. Chuck makes Wilson his friend, he talks to him, laughs with him and he unloads all his frustrations, affection, rage and powelesness on Wilson. That is how he manages to survive emotionally.

When we suffer a loss, be it from a love relationship, work or our health, we feel alone: as if we were abandoned on a lonely island. The pain is so intense that we can feel it physically. We cannot think, we do not reason or analyze, we are so immersed in the pain that the mind is in a daze and we do not have any control over our thoughts and emotions. If we think that life does not make sense anymore, the body reacts according to that thought and we start to somatize (transform emotional problems into physical symptoms). That is when we say that "our soul hurts."

Why do we feel pain? Because of a delusion of the mind: the thought that things are forever. One of the fundamentals of Buddhism is that everything is transitory and "impermanent." When we cling to people, material possessions or situations, when we lose them, we feel this devastating pain which clouds understanding because we do not want to let go. Recognizing that nothing is permanent is a way of dealing with pain. There are always changes, and the biggest one is emotional or physical death. When we are confronted with an event of such magnitude, it is necessary to be able to accept the circumstances. Once something changes, the experience will never be the same. That is when we have to reflect, analyze, accept, let go and work on the change.

Crying wisely and consciously frees and heals. Doing it this way cleans our aura (magnetic field) and our chakras. What is crying consciously? It is taking time to cry, not being submerged in suffering, to know that later comes calm, and to be confident that the pain is going to subside. It is a matter of time and patience, reasoning and understanding that it is necessary to devote yourself to God or the Universe. We have to recognize that in our pain there is growth and strength: after the dark night comes dawn. If we learn what experience teaches us we are reborn to a new and better state of consciousness. There are two questions that you can analyze and reflect about: What do I have to learn from this experience? Do I have to let go, learn to really love, to have more compassion? The answer will help you to work on the loss.

An ancient legend tells the story of a king who wanted to govern his emotions. He was looking for something that made him feel peace and tranquility every time he looked at it. He met with all the wise men of his kingdom and they started the search. They found a wise Sufi man who gave them a ring, telling them: *"There is only one condition, give the ring to the king and tell him to only look at the underside of the stone when he feels that everything is lost, that his agony is untenable and when he feels completely powerless to deal with the circumstances; if he does not do that, he will miss the message."* The king obeyed, and some time later he lost his kingdom. He had to abandon all his riches, his family and all he had in order to save his life. While he was fleeing his horse died and he continued running until he reached an abyss from where apparently there was no way out. At that moment he remembered the ring, he looked under the stone and there was the message: "THIS TOO SHALL PASS."

It is not important in what kind of situation you are right now, but remember "THIS TOO SHALL PASS."

One evening around 11:00 o'clock I received a phone call. My heart jumped and according to what I had learned I thought that "something bad" had happened. Immediately I decided that this "something" was good and so I answered the phone affirming that "only the best manifests itself in my life." It was Sofia, she had read one of my articles published in El Nuevo Día and she wanted to contact me. She was suffering from the loss of her partner after 15 years, and she felt lost, confused, in pain. She wanted to work on the loss, but she felt too much resentment, pain and despair. She did not know what to do. She did not have any children, and so she could not take refuge in them - as many people do. She was so desperate that we met the next day and she started working.

When she saw the Mandala for Transformation she told me: *"I cannot fill this out like this, I have to take it home and think about it very well." I answered her : "If that is what you want, fine. But it would be good if you could start working immediately.* "After a long silence she decided that she would fill it out, but with my help. She had a lot of doubts and she did not know at which number of each area she was, so she started with the Relationship area (remember you can start with the area you want). I asked her how satisfied she was in this area, with number one being the one of least satisfaction and number ten the one of most satisfaction. Her answer was "zero," but that number is not on the wheel. For me it is not possible to imagine that someone believes to be in zero; even though I have learned that there are moments when the pain is so intense that it is possible to be in "minus zero." She put "minus zero." Later she indicated the other areas which were also very low (between the numbers 1 and 4).

The first reading I recommended to her was "You can heal your Life" by Louise Hay. This book has exercises and we agreed that she would do them all. This was going to be an intense process and a great desire and effort was necessary from her side so that she could get out of the turmoil she was in. She learned to meditate and to visualize. She spent all of her first working week reading, meditating, visualizing and writing in her journal. She was not a practitioner of

Hatha Yoga, so she decided that her pose would be Sukhasana, or the easy pose. I taught her how to do it so that she would be comfortable during her reconstruction process. She worked intensely, she read incessantly and she did all the tasks we designed together.

While she was involved in her process of change she was able to see that her partner had a drinking problem, something she had refused to believe. She was in denial for so many years that she thought that to drink "socially" (as he called it) was acceptable. However when he drank, his conduct changed and he abused her emotionally. With time and without noticing she became codependent.

She mistook codependence for unconditional love. When we are in this kind of love, a sensation of great peace, calm and equanimity emerges from our heart. In unconditional love we do not make exceptions of people, we see the universal energy of love in everybody. This is compassionate love that great teachers like Buddha, Jesus Christ, Gandhi, Mother Teresa of Calcutta and many others came to teach us.

Loving kindness is the energy of the highest frequency vibration and it blooms within all human beings because our nature is love. As we synchronize with it, it starts flowing through our thoughts, actions and words. Loving kindness protects us from hate, jealousy and the damage that low frequency thoughts can cause us. When we allow this energy to emanate from our heart it starts to change us and transforms everything around us.

In unconditional love you move to help others without taking into consideration who they are or what they look like, you only see a being of light, full of love energy. True love makes us give the best of ourselves without expecting anything in return. We have the capacity to give because we want to help and be useful. Respect, admiration and compassion are characteristics of unconditional love. When you truly love someone you feel respect, admiration, sweetness, kindness towards that person and you are happy.

If we suffer in a love relationship, it is necessary to analyze and reflect about if what we feel is love or dependence. In unconditional love the only thing we wish for is the wellbeing of the loved one, we wish this person happiness. In a dependency situation we do not conceive life without him or her, we cannot reason and we think that if this person is not with us anymore, life would have no sense. It is necessary to pay attention to these signals because we could become victims of codependence or addiction to love. When this happens, fear of losing the love of our partner makes us accept and stay in abusive or dysfunctional relationships. In these cases it is necessary to look for professional help, because there is a tendency to give up power and continue to suffer instead of freeing ourselves. Loving unconditionally does not mean being abused.

It is important to internalize that the first unconditional love is towards ourselves. In order to be able to love others we first have to learn to love ourselves, not with an egotistic-narcissistic love where only we are important: I, me, mine, with me; but with loving kindness that permits us to respect ourselves, see all our qualities, accept ourselves the way we are and not delude ourselves when we notice that something has to be improved. When we accept ourselves the way we are we open the door to a change in our lives. When we love unconditionally we get closer to God because God is love.

Supreme Master Ching Hai says that "*in this ephemeral life we too are God. When we love our children, neighbors and friends we represent God's qualities. We develop love in ourselves and we express it through our actions.*"

Sofia discovered that what she was feeling was not true love. She frequently thought that she did not have an identity of her own because she was always trying to please her partner and she felt guilty when he was not satisfied. Sometimes she got very angry with herself for not getting out of the cycle of suffering. She understood that she had become a victim of a very subtle emotional abuse. Her partner did not attack her physically but he frequently made degrading comments to her. The most surprising thing about this case is that she is a high-ranking professional in a private company and made much more money than he did. Her work made her travel at least two or three times a year, something that bothered him a lot. The higher she ranked in her profession, the more expletives he used towards her.

How could such a successful woman let herself be abused that way? Because of fear. Fear of being alone, what people would say, fear of not finding *"the love of her life."* She had an exceptional cognitive intelligence but her emotional intelligence was nearly zero. On the other hand, in her eagerness to make the relationship work she wanted to control everything, and that caused big fights. She decided where they would go for dinner, what movie they were going to see and where they would spend their vacations. She always found a way to manipulate the situation and have things her way. She had been so verbally abused that she felt very hurt and unconsciously she tried to retaliate controlling everything. That desire for control is part of codependent behavior. It is the desire to control everything, but at the same time there is a feeling of fear, desperation and guilt.

Sofia took immediate action to work on her change and she did it without stopping. It took her nearly two years to be able to say that she felt "liberated" and that she was a new woman. She did not despair and she did not hurry the process. She did all the recommended reading and exercises. Her process filled her with a lot of satisfaction and now she assures that she feels "fulfilled as a woman." She and her partner took couple therapy sessions and were able to save their relationship.

We always have to understand that our actions speak more than a thousand words. If you act with love, you receive love. Imagine what life would be like if all of our actions were moved by love and compassion. That would finally make us achieve peace on this planet.

MEDITATION

Love meditation is very powerful and it is the best armor against dependency and poisons of the mind. Look for a quiet place, away from noise, disconnect all you phones. Sit down comfortably, close your eyes and breathe deeply several times. Think of the love you feel for all your loved ones, expand this love energy to all living beings, including those you have considered your enemies.

Imagine yourself as a great loving energy and affirm in your mind that: all beings are full of Unconditional Love Energy. Continue breathing while imagining all of them filled with love. When you think it is enough time, open your eyes slowly and experience love in your heart.

YOGA

The pose recommended for this area is The Warrior I. Look for page 270 in the Yoga poses section for instructions and practice it every day.

TAROT

Sit down comfortably with the 22 Major Arcana cards. Do a spread and take out a card, this is the archetype that will help you to work on this area. Look for the meaning of the card in the section provided for it (see pages 176-256). Write in your journal the meaning that this card has for you at this moment.

MEDITATIVE COACHING

1. On what occasions do you think you are responsible of other people's actions?
2. What situations make you help others without them having asked for it?
3. How many times do you hear yourself saying yes when you really want to say no?
4. When do guilt symptoms determine your priorities?
5. How long does it take you to get out of the vicious cycle of destructive thoughts ?

6. How can you recognize a healthy relationship?
7. How willing are you to surrender everything to God or your Higher Self?
8. How willing are you to take action to get out of the codependence you live in?
9. How many times a week do you try to cultivate your relationships?
10. What steps do you have to take to build new relationships?

MEDITATIVE WRITING (THE JOURNAL)

Write in your journal any image, sound, color or sensation you experienced during meditation. If any information came to you, or you understood or received answers to any of your concerns, write them down in your journal and study them. Also write the answers to the Meditative Coaching questions and reflect about each of them. Do not forget that you decide the time you dedicate to this process, you can answer one or several questions. It is your decision.

AFFIRMATIONS

- *I only attract to my life people who help me in my self-realization process.*
- *I am willing to let go and leave any relationship that does not honor who I am.*
- *I have new and wonderful relationships with everything around me.*
- *I feel unconditional love. I give and receive unconditional love.*
- *I am thankful for the loving presence of everybody in my life.*
- *God's Divine Love works through me to have quality relationships.*

VISUALIZATION

Lie down comfortably at a place where nothing disturbs you. Close your eyes and visualize yourself in the confidence and love relationships you have always longed for. Take your time, visualize every detail in the relationship. How you want it to be, what you want to happen, what qualities you want the person to have and how you want things to go.

ACTION

Answer the questions of meditative coaching, reflect about your answers and think what small big step you can take this week. For example: join a codependency support group. If you want to socialize more look for groups where you can have inter-dependent relationships (reciprocal dependence) like Yoga, Tai Chi and spiritual or development and emotional growth groups among others. Also ask yourself: How is my disposition to help? If you feel you want to be useful and help those who need it most, look for a place where you can offer your services. This is something that always increases our energy and makes us feel better about ourselves.

During this week try to help others, start with your family. If you have something you want to work with them, that is the correct moment.

Take action, that is what determines triumph in your process.

Recommended reading:

Codependent no more	Melodie Beattie
Emotional Intelligence	Daniel Goleman
Take Time For Your Life	Cheryl Richardson
When Things fall apart	Pema Chödrön
The Power of Verbal Intelligence	Tony Buzan

Intimate/ Social Relationships

Relationships that empower me

are the ones that make me feel filled with energy.

In my relationships I connect with the

Marvelous Energy of the Universe.

My relationships are a reflex of my inner self,

I honor them and they honor me.

¡¡¡ Glory to God!!!

¡¡¡ Glory to the Infinite Universe!!!

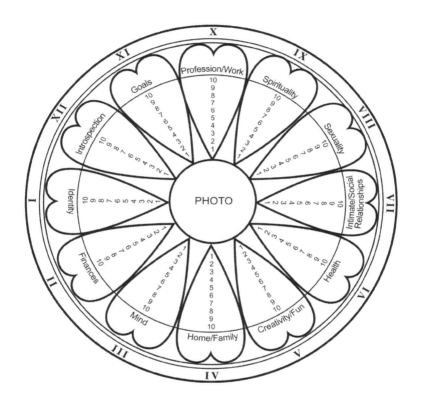

AREA VIII
SEXUALITY

Area VIII

SEXUALITY

As you might have noticed, throughout this book you have been consistently asked: "What is (this or that) for you?" and "What does (this or that) mean to you?" I insist on asking you these questions because everything in life deals with what a certain situation or concept mean to you. That is why I ask you: "What does sexuality mean to you?" "How do you define it?"

Some people think that sexuality is only the sex act or that it is simply sex. For others it includes several areas of their life. While for some people sexuality includes from sensuality and initial flirtation to the sex act itself, for others it is the satisfaction to be comfortable with the person they chose as their partner.

Due to lack of information we associate sex- many times -with something bad or impure. It is convenient to understand that this association is incorrect. When we love, sex is the best thing God has given us, it is the epitome of creation. That is why master Osho says in his book *Tantra, Spirituality and Sex* "that in order to enjoy its high frequency vibration and have a full and satisfactory life "*sex has to become love*". Using sexual energy wisely can transmute (change from one form into another) many situations in your life.

Some people proclaim that "sex is not everything." Maybe it is that way for them because they chose a celibate lifestyle. This is admirable because it requires a great preparation through meditation and praying.

But if we have not chosen this for ourselves, we have to understand that sexual desire should not be eliminated or repressed, even though it is not possible to unleash lust because that could lead you to unconsciousness. If you do not have self-control over your sexual energy, you do not honor your values or the temple that is your body. It is possible that you do not even consider that sexually transmitted diseases exist. Sexual energy needs an escape valve because it is like water, it always tries to get out. We have to be conscious that this valve is one that honors the spiritual path we have chosen. For some this escape valve could be masturbation, while for others it can be fasting and prayer. It could also be writing, dancing, singing. Explore the alternatives that vibrate with you.

This energy is something natural that is born with us. It is present from childhood on and stays with us through our life. The American writer Napoleon Hill, tells us in his book *Think and Grow Rich* *"sexual desire is the most powerful of human desires"* and if we use it conscientiously we can reach our goals. Sexual energy is so great and powerful that we are able to create a human being through the loving sex act. If we can create human life we can also create what we desire, provided it is synchronized to the high love vibration and it benefits everybody.

Maria Mercedes had been working on Area VII (Relationships) around one month. In her case the relationship with her partner was the one that gave her the most challenges. When she reviewed the Mandala for Transformation (it is recommended to do this every 21 days, every three month or every time you feel the need to see how your energy is in each of the areas) Maria Mercedes put a mark on number two in the Sexuality Area and number four in the Relationship area, which indicated that her sexual energy was very low and the relationship with her partner needed an infusion of energy. She had not taken into consideration that when she increased energy in the sexual area maybe the relationship with her mate would improve also.

She had been educated in a school for girls and her parents were very religious. In one of our sessions she remembered that they had hit her because they surprised her touching "herself intimately." That marked her so much that she never touched herself again (even less looking at her naked body in the mirror) unless she was taking a bath. She was very repressed regarding her sexuality and she did not even know what an orgasm was; it was very difficult for her to talk about this topic but her love for her partner was so great that she was determined to confront her fears in order to save her relationship.

She could also see that Area II (finances/money) was low (she had put a mark on 4). I explained to her that Area VIII (sexuality) is just in front of Area II and so there is a reciprocal energy among the two. Usually if one of these areas is low the other one will be too. If Area number II is low on energy it is necessary to take action and increase it, even if it is only one level so that Area number VIII does not remain without energy and is not affected. Equally, when Area VIII is low, Area II feels the impact.

Together we prepared an action plan to increase the energy of her second chakra – which is sexuality, and also the money chakra – which included Master Osho's Dynamic Meditation (see description in the Instrument section). She worked with quartzes, clay poultices on the indicated area and visited her gynecologist to see if there was any medical condition affecting her because she felt discomfort on penetration. She dismissed the possibility of a physical condition (because she did well on her medical examination) and she dedicated time to educate herself regarding her sexuality. What did sex mean to her? She discovered that it was for procreation and that her deep religious beliefs had taken her to think that sex was only to "create and multiply." She read several books, she got informed and made an appointment with a sexologist to deal with her fears. Her husband helped her and they were able to improve their sexual relations to be satisfactory for both of them. Today Maria Mercedes enjoys her orgasms and does not feel guilty about it. She understood that this is the culmination of the love that she and her husband felt as a couple and she converted her sexual experience into a spiritual one, because at the moment of orgasm both visualized themselves united in the Love of the Universe and they were able to feel what it is to vibrate together.

MEDITATION

For this meditation separate at least 20 minutes in your agenda. Look for a quiet place without interruptions and disconnect all phones. Sit down in Sukhasana (easy pose) and close your eyes. Put your attention on the second chakra. Observe what you feel or see. Inhale deeply and visualize a white light coming up from your first chakra until it goes out at the seventh (the crown). Feel how this energy bathes all your body. When you finish meditation get your journal.

YOGA

The recommended pose for this area is The Cobra. If you are a beginner in Hatha Yoga practice, look for the recommended pose on page 272.

TAROT

Take the 22 Major Arcana cards. Pick one of the recommended spreads and observe what card the Tarot shows you. This is the archetype that will help you to work on this area. Look for the meaning of the card in the section provided for it (see pages 176-256) and after looking up the definition write in your journal the meaning it has for you at the moment.

MEDITATIVE COACHING

1. What does sexuality mean to me?
2. How do I feel sexually?
3. How satisfied am I with my sexual performance?
4. When was the last time I had an orgasm? How would I describe it?
5. What has to happen in order to have a pleasurable sexual relation?
6. How can I use my sexual energy satisfactorily?
7. What is my favorite moment for making love?
8. How guilty do I feel for having sexual/love relations?
9. What voice from the past tells me that I cannot enjoy loving sex?
10. What images come to my mind and how do I feel?

MEDITATIVE WRITING (THE JOURNAL)

Write down any image, sound, color or sensation that you experienced during meditation.

Write the answers to the Meditative Coaching questions and reflect about each of them. If you feel you need to look for the help of a sexologist, call and make an appointment immediately.

AFFIRMATIONS

- Making love (having sexual relations) is good and pleasurable.
- I accept that I deserve to enjoy the energy I feel when I have an orgasm.
- I am willing to change my perception of what sex is.
- I enjoy every day and every moment I make love.
- My orgasms are my connection with the Divine.

VISUALIZATION/MASTURBATION

Lie down comfortably and make sure that you will not be interrupted. Close your eyes, visualize yourself having the most beautiful and satisfactory loving sexual relation of your life. Use all your senses. Touch all your body while you imagine that this energy you are liberating will help you to manifest your goals. Continue feeling the energy and at the moment of orgasm visualize yourself reaching the life of your dreams.

ACTION

If you have a partner, agree on the time you can be alone (if you have children look for someone to take care of them) At the moment of orgasm visualize the goals you have reached. If you do not have a partner, do the visualization/masturbation at least once a week or at the frequency you think is necessary for you. At the moment of orgasm visualize that all your desires are coming true.

Recommended Reading:

Tantra, Spirituality and Sex   Osho
Tantra the Art of Living   Marc Allen
The Art of Sexual Ecstasy   Margo Anand
The Art of Sexual Magic   Margo Anand
Creative Visualization   Shakti Gawain

Sexuality

The juices of life

flow over me, they fill me with life,

they keep me young and vigorous.

I enjoy every moment and I move

in celebration of

my roaring orgasm.

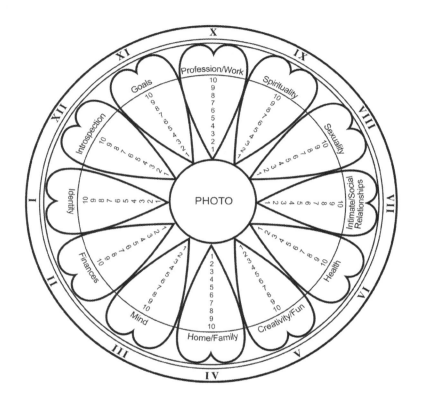

AREA IX
SPIRITUALITY

Area IX

SPIRITUALITY

All religions are united by love. BHAMA

During the time I have been working with the Yoga-Tarot for Transformation methodology I have noticed that there are three areas which people are most preoccupied with: love, money and health. Even though, the area I consider the most transcendental is spirituality and I noticed that it is not given the importance it deserves.

Spirituality can be defined as the connection with this power greater than all of us, which moves everything, unites everything, sustains everything and what everything is made of.

The connection with this Superior Power defines everything else in our lives. The way we are, how we relate to what surrounds us, how we manage our health, our finances, our work, our family, etc. Everything in life is intimately tied to this connection.

Without this union we cannot undertake the journey that is our life. It is like being in an airplane without a pilot and without course. We would travel without a Control Tower to indicate our final destination to us. Also, if we do not have the necessary instruments for our journey through life (Meditation, Consciousness of a Superior Being, Honoring life) we have no aim and we feel disoriented. Sometimes we try hard to achieve health, money and love, but we feel alone, empty and we live life adrift and lost.

Some of the sentences I heard from people who are healthy, have money, love and success are: *"I feel an emptiness that I cannot define," "even if I have a beautiful family, good health and a prosperous financial situation, I feel lonely,"* etc. These people do not realize that this emptiness can only be filled by our union with God, or what you consider Divine Energy or a Superior Being.

In the "Spirituality and Healing" workshops by Harvard University the importance of the connection with Divinity in our lives is constantly mentioned. Dr. Herbert Benson, a pioneer in scientifically proving the benefits of meditation and presenter in the workshops, shared with a group of doctors and scientists their studies about the importance of a spiritual connection in human life.

A human being always believes in something: an Energy, a Superior Being, God. Dr. Wayne Dyer, an American motivational speaker and writer, says first it is necessary to believe and then see. If you believe that God (Divinity, your superior Being, Devine Intelligence or the name you want to give it) is always in charge of your life and everything that happens is for your greatest benefit, you can see and appreciate that Divinity is in everything around you and continues to work in your life every day. Meditate, ask for direction and recognize that here and now is a good time to start your relationship with the Divine Energy of the Universe.

In the "Spirituality and Healing" workshops by Harvard University I understood Dr. Puchalsky defined spirituality as: *"That part of our being that desires a meaning in life, to know that it has a purpose, that there is hope in the middle of chaos and desolation, that looks for pardon and freedom. Spirituality can be expressed in philosophical, religious or personal believes, terms that integrate values and ethical codes of conduct in a person. Spirituality is that part of the human being which tries to understand who we are in this vast Universe and what our purpose in life is."*

When we feel connected with this Fountain of Life we experience an inexpressible energy and interior peace, difficult to explain in words. In Tao Te Ching Lao Tzu tells us that *"The Tao that can be named is not the Tao."* We cannot explain who or what God is. We can only feel and experience it and when we do it the Universe becomes our center and direction and everything we do we do it because of or for Him/Her.

In this connection we experience ecstasy, peace, joy and vitality, independently of what is going on in our lives at the moment. Always, even at the most difficult moments, when we speak to God and communicate with Him/Her, we discover that the burden gets less heavy because we know – as Hindu master Dada Vaswani says – *"God is always in charge."* There is nothing to fear, He/She is always with us along the whole journey and on the spiritual road we choose.

It would be good if you could distinguish between religion and spirituality. For me religion are the guidelines and rules we have to follow to please God. It is a system of believes we have been taught and the map we are given to find the way (in Christian religions Jesus Christ is the way). When we find our way and follow directions we will get to that place (Heaven) we have been promised. In spirituality we change our conscience in a way where structures are perceived as ties, and they are broken. There are no rules or commandments, only eternal love for the Universe/God/the Superior Being and for our brothers. That is the time when we truly live Jesus Christ's words: *"love each other the way I have loved you"* and *"love your neighbor as yourself."* We see divinity in everything and everybody, we honor that infinite love. We live in this indescribable light and we experience what God is for me: Compassionate love.

In all religions there are norms, rules or mandates that guide us in a better coexistence with our planetary brothers. When we think that we disobeyed some of these rules, guidelines or commandments we feel dishonest, impure and we think that *"God is going to punish us."* What voice of the past stays in our mind and makes us think that we are separated from this superior force? Most of the time it is guilt.

Our system of believes – taught during our childhood – made us think that if we do something "bad" (we did not comply with some of the rules or commandments) God will punish us, and many times we prefer to get away from Him/Her instead of keeping connected. However this estrangement is only in our mind, God is always with us because we are of his same nature. It is not important what we do, this Superior Energy is always within us, it never leaves us. Separation does not exist. We are at one with the Universe and with everything around us.

This does not mean that we should live life "crazily" without taking other people into consideration. The principle of peace is respecting and honoring everybody and everything, the way we will respect and honor ourselves. In order to do that it is essential to love ourselves unconditionally, because nobody can give what he/she does not have.

The Universe, God or this force that some people cannot explain, communicates through a feeling or emotion originated by unconditional love and compassion without ego and without judgment. It is the ego and judging of others that makes us feel distant from this Unconditional Love. When our ego tells us that something is "bad" or we judge someone, this energy gets affected and we feel empty without being able to recognize what is happening to us.

That is how Josué Antonio felt when he came to see me. Even with an excellent job (he was a senior executive of a company in Miami which made him travel to Puerto Rico frequently) with a beautiful family, and he and his wife loved each other. He had healthy and beautiful girls but even though he felt a great emptiness. He thought that he had a severe depression and he had seen several psychologists and psychiatrists without being able to fill his emptiness or understand what was happening to him. He had everything that any person desired to be happy: health, success, money and love, but he felt that he was missing something and he could not define what it was.

When he filled out the Mandala for Transformation and we checked the numbers he had put a mark on in each area I noticed that the Spirituality area was on number one. I explained to him that the most important areas in each human being's life are: Spirituality (Area IX), (Identity Area I), Mind (Area III) and Introspection (Area XII). Of all these areas Spirituality is the most important one, because the way we face our challenges depends on it. In Josué Antonio's case the Identity, Mind and Introspection Areas were also low on energy. He could not understand that how it was possible that he was so successful in his life while the relationship with himself was not what he longed for.

When we started working he was very disciplined (one of the qualities that had made him successful) and he did all the recommended reading. He did all his meditations, and every day for 21 days he did the complete system we had designed together. At the end of the stipulated time he came to the conclusion that he had emulated his father. His father was in the military and Josué Antonio had acquired discipline and consistence to do what was necessary to obtain his goals. Nevertheless in his childhood he practically never heard the word of God and even less teachings to cultivate his spirituality. As a consequence these topics were new to him.

He discovered that he was implacable with people who did not think or do things the way he understood they had to be done. He judged everybody and criticized relentlessly. He was not tolerant with those who —according to him – were neither intelligent nor diligent. He was predominant occasionally and his wife had brought to his attention this lack of compassion that made her feel uncomfortable.

He was loving with his family, but he did not have the sensibility to recognize when a situation needed the connection with Divinity. His daughters were baptized in the catholic faith and he had to attend classes previous to baptism. At that moment he understood that something superior to him existed, but he could not figure out what it was. He attended the first communion of each of his daughters, enjoying seeing them smiling and happy, but personally he had not been able to *"be born again."*

Once I heard someone say that God is one and so merciful that He/She created many ways to get to Him/Her and that our journey is totally individual. We always have to meditate and ask to be shown ours. For Josué Antonio the way was meditation, communion with nature, prayer and introspection. During one of his meditations he could feel peace, joy and the energy that is felt experiencing Superior Energy. He understood that all of us are made of the same energy and that everyone has talents and does the best possible with what is available at the moment.

When he did the meditation about Love Extension (which we are going to explain later on) he understood that he could extend the love he felt for his family to everybody around him and that he could be more compassionate and loving. He did a *"love demonstration exercise"* for a week. That included smiling and greeting people he did not know up to buying food for a homeless man. At the end of the week he felt happy and satisfied with himself. He joined a social welfare program to give service to those who most needed it. He discovered that when he gave of his abundance the Universe compensated him more abundantly. He never thought he could be that happy and consciously enjoy all the blessings he had. He is joyful now and one can say that *"he experienced God, he experienced love of himself and of others."*

MEDITATION

For this meditation set aside at least 20 minutes in your agenda. Look for a quiet place where nothing interrupts you and disconnect the phones. Lie down in the Savasana pose (Relaxation– page 269) and close your eyes. Put your attention on the seventh chakra. Breathe deeply and observe your respiration. Feel the peace, feel God's energy in all your body. When you inhale, repeat: *"God is love"* and when you exhale, repeat: *'I am love."* At the end of the 20 minutes breathe in deeply and open your eyes little by little, saying:

"God is here, with me and within me." (If in the spiritual journey you have chosen there is another word for God, use it. You can say something like: *"The Divine Energy is here, with me and within me"* or *"The Universe is here, with me and within me.)."*

YOGA

Do the Lotus or half Lotus pose (page 273) which is recommended for this area. If you practice Hatha Yoga, use your intuition and do the pose that comes to your mind and which your heart indicates to you. The Universe always supports you and you will see the pose, it will show itself to you. If you do not practice Hatha Yoga, look for a nice place and meditate; you are already in Yoga (Union).

TAROT

Sit down comfortably with the 22 Major Arcana cards. Pick one of the recommended spreads and observe which card the Tarot shows you. This is the archetype that will help you to work on this area. Look up the meaning of the card in the section provided for it (see pages 176-256) After looking up the definition write in your journal the meaning that this card has for you at this moment.

MEDITATIVE COACHING

1. What does God mean to me?
2. What can I do to experience God?
3. How satisfied am I with the spiritual journey I chose?
4. How do I connect with God or with this superior force within me?
   How would I describe it?
5. What makes me think that I did something "bad"?
6. How often do I judge others and myself?

7. How often do I give love, including to myself?
8. How guilty do I feel when I did something that makes me feel disconnected from this Divine Energy?
9. What can I do to remember that I am a Being of Light and activate the Divine Energy within me again?
10. What images come to my mind when I think of the Universe and how do I feel?

MEDITATIVE WRITING (THE JOURNAL)

Write down any image, sound, color or sensation you experienced during meditation. Write down the answers to the Meditative Coaching questions and reflect about each of them.

VISUALIZATION (Extend love)

Lie down at a comfortable place where you will not be interrupted. Breathe and enter into a state of deep relaxation. Visualize love irradiating from your heart. Feel how everything touched by love is reborn and flourishes. Extend love energy to all loved ones; to anybody who needs love and compassion. When you finish extending this marvelous energy, visualize it coming back to your heart multiplied. Inhale deeply and open your eyes slowly. Give thanks because everybody touched by love is healthy and joyful.

AFFIRMATIONS

- I am one with the Universe.
- God is Love.
- God is within me and I am within Him/Her.
- The Divine Energy sustains me.
- Every day and every hour I enjoy my connection with God more.
- The Light of the Universe lives in me.

ACTION

For one week smile at everybody. God is everywhere, so when you smile at others you are smiling at Him/Her.

Recommended reading:

The Experience of God	Johnathan Robinson
The Divine Matrix	Gregg Braden
One Day My Soul Just Opened Up	Iyanla Vanzant
Practicing the Path	Yangsi Rinpoche
How to know God	Deepak Chopra
Basics of Buddhism	Pat Allwright
The Buddha in your Mirror	Woody Hochswender, Gregg Martin and Ted Morino

Spirituality

In the Divine Connection with the Universe

I rejoice in God's Love.

I rejoice in the Love of Divinity.

God is love and I enjoy Him/Her in love.

And He/She enjoys me.

We are one.

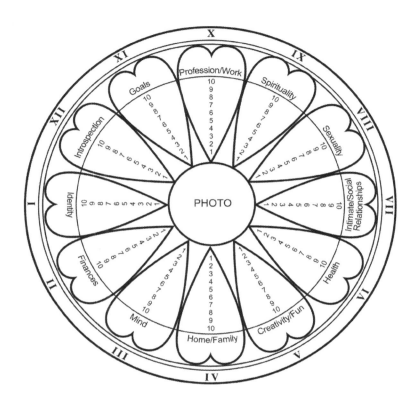

AREA X
PROFESSION/WORK

MA PREM BHAMA

Area X

WORK/PROFESSION

Most of the religions in the world express that the human being is inherently good. In Buddhism the teaching is that Buddha nature is within all of us. We are beings of light. That is the reason why nearly every human being's greatest aspirations are : be able to help others, do something memorable to help the human race and leave a legacy for which to be remembered. However, many times because of a poisoned mind people do things that consternate us and make us think that there are more people asleep than doing things to benefit others.

Unfortunately the media cover more events that discourage us than those where the human being considers himself/herself a being of light, and we make a mistake thinking that *this world is going to end'*. I once read that the Dalai Lama said that for each negative event there are thousands of positive ones happening, but they are not getting the recognition they deserve.

Within the framework of the mentioned aspirations we have asked ourselves many times what the true purpose of life is and why we have come to this planet. Sometimes deep within ourselves we desire to be useful and change the world. We long for peace, happiness and abundance, not only for ourselves but for everybody living on Mother Earth.

When we were children we might have dreamt of being doctors, lawyers, policemen, firefighters, governors o engineers. To have a profession where we could help others and at the same time be successful and earn much money. Maybe it did not cross our mind that any profession or occupation we carry out with love and passion will be beneficial for everybody.

That is why we sometimes do things we do not like, do not fulfill or impassion us. What makes a "professional" different from a person "without a profession"? According to the Dictionary of the Royal Spanish Academy a professional is someone who practices a profession, a word which is defined as *"action and effect of professing."* And what is professing? The Royal Academy says that it is *"practicing a science, an art, a profession, etc."* That means that in one way or another we are all professionals because we do something in exchange for a salary.

University studies help to differentiate the cognitive level of people who finished a career from those who did not. However there is no guarantee that a university diploma gives a person the title of a *"good professional"*. I have met men and women with the highest university titles who emotionally had a lot to learn. On the other hand, life with its teachings - if we know how to profit from them – can educate us for a higher purpose. It teaches us the necessary lessons to learn to love unconditionally. This is the great lesson that has to be learned because if not, life, the Universe or however you want to call it, will consistently repeat the same challenges so that we learn how to love. For me the most beautiful teaching is to learn how to love compassionately, including ourselves.

It is necessary to read, study, get informed to be able to do the job or occupation we have chosen. This is the way we can offer our knowledge in exchange of energy which could be money, goods or a service. However, even with all the university titles in the world we find ourselves working at something we do not like or does not satisfy us due to the simple fact of making *"a lot of money."* There are people who end up being professionals with a very low vibration frequency and they do not dedicate the necessary love or attention to their profession.

It is important to ask yourself and reflect about if you see your work as an art and if you feel love for what you do. If you perceive it like an art and love it, you are a person doing what you like to do and therefore you are vibrating at a high frequency in this area of your life. If, on the other hand, a job that you do to receive a salary does not satisfy you, does not fulfill you or does not make you happy, this is a good moment for you to meditate and decide if you want to continue with this dilemma or if you want to change. Many times we prefer to stay the way we are because it is easier and no effort is required. An advice that writer and conference speaker Jack Canfield gives in his book *The Success Principles* is that you have to stop doing two things in order to get yourself out of the spider web you are in and see at least a small change in your life: complain and blame others.

When you complain that :" *I am tired of this job*", "*I cannot go on like this*", *I want a different job*", your energy level decreases more and more, up to a point when you feel that you do not want to get up to go to work. When you do go, you do it without enthusiasm or without joy, life stinks and you will hinder the others in their work. When you blame others, you are not taking responsibility for your life and you do not want to recognize that only you can make the decision to change. The law of Karma says that every cause has an effect, or as we have heard before: you reap what you sow. The first step to reconstruct your life is to accept responsibility for your actions, it is the only way to move towards what you want to achieve.

Many times we have heard about living life with a purpose. Do you know yours? If I asked you what it is to live a life with a purpose, would you know the answer? (Stop what you are doing at the moment and meditate for at least 20 minutes, reflect and continue reading). A purpose is *the reason for which something is done or created or for which something exists* and is an intention a person has to do or achieve something. What do you want to achieve in your life? Most of the people want to be rich and famous, but are they willing to accept or work on the change that this entails?

The answers to these questions make many people sabotage themselves while trying it. They unconsciously do not want to expose their private life, nor do they want to invest the hours of effort that requires, so they prefer to stay the way they are and later they complain and blame others: life *"because it has not been good to me;"* money *"because if I had more I could do what I wanted;"* or their family members *"because they do not support me;"* and number one: their parents *"because they did not dedicate enough time to me and they mistreated me."* But it is not possible to blame the parents or others all your life. It is time to accept our responsibility and make an effort to change.

People who spend their life complaining about others and their personal circumstances have not understood that if we really try to reach a goal, all our efforts become joyful because we know that all this energy we are investing is going to materialize what we want. However you have to be aware that you and only you have to do this.

Francisco José came to me referred by someone I do not know, but who had heard about the work I was doing with my clients and he/she thought that I could help him. He was at a stage in his life where he did not know what to do. He did not feel like going to work and he looked for all possible excuses not to do so. He had a well-paying job at a well-known law firm and he was so sure that he liked what he was doing that he decided to study law. When the "domino got stuck" was when he was not able to pass the bar exam for the second time. He arrived without hope and he did not know which way to go.

The first thing I told him was to breathe. Breathing is the most important thing in our lives. We can be without eating for many days, maybe one month. We can live without water for maybe three days, but without air - oxygen- we do not live more than three minutes. Maybe someone trained in that aspect could resist five minutes, but I do not think more than that. When we want to relax, the fastest way is inhaling and putting attention on exhalation. Later I explained to him how to meditate and then he filled out the Mandala for Transformation. His Mandala seemed like a flat tire, his energy was very low in all areas, a consequence of his uncertainty and frustration.

When he answered the Meditative Coaching (What is the purpose of my life and what do I want to achieve?) he understood that what he really wanted to do was to help people transcend their challenges. He unconsciously had a limiting belief regarding the career he had chosen to study. Since childhood he had been told that lawyers and doctors only worked to make money and did not care about what their clients felt. After several coaching sessions he understood that that could happen in any profession. The important thing was not what he did, but how he did it and how he felt doing it. He came to the conclusion that when he would do his job he would do everything necessary to help his clients.

However, even after what he had found out, he felt that he had not hit the nail on the head. There was still something that had to be integrated and he did not know what it was. Our work together lasted more than two years and as the saying goes: *"A happy outcome is worth waiting for."* After eight months of consistent work, he understood during a meditation that what he really wanted was to study psychology. He understood that apart from helping people with his knowledge of the law he could also help them having a better quality of life. *"What is necessary to allow this happen?"* I asked him. *"Look for information and find out where I can study the topic of my passion."* *"How long will it take you to do this?"* I asked him. *"Tomorrow"* he answered. We agreed that he would call me to tell me which small big step he had taken. The next day he called me to tell me that he had enrolled and would start his psychology studies.

Francisco José put marks on his Mandala again and he saw that his energy had increased. He felt happy, satisfied and enthusiastic with what he was going to undertake. Now he saw his work as something that helped him make his dream come true and he would get up happy to go to work and with a different attitude.

When we acknowledge that nothing is permanent we can see that the job we do is the springboard that helps us to reach our goals. Let us give thanks because the money energy the job provides is a vehicle to make our dreams come true. When we put our attention on what we want to achieve we can get up happy to go to work because we know that our dreams will become reality.

Francisco José decided to continue his studies in the United States. He used to come and go until he decided to stay away and work out of Puerto Rico. I know that at present he is living the "life of his dreams" and helping many people transcend their challenges.

MEDITATION

Set aside 20 minutes for this meditation. Make sure you will not be interrupted. Look for a quiet place and disconnect the telephones. Lie down in Savasana (Relaxation pose – page 269) and close your eyes. Start a conscious breathing process. Inhale deeply until you feel that your stomach and your rib cage expand. Continue inhaling until you feel that the collar bones lift up. Stop breathing and count up to six (if it is a challenge for you, breathe normally) exhale slowly counting up to six and when you have exhaled completely count up to six again. Inhale, following the same rhythm for three cycles. Now inhale deeply and then breathe normally. Ask God, the Universe, your Superior Being (or how you want to call him/her) What is my purpose in life? Where can I be most beneficial? Continue inhaling and focus on the answer.

YOGA

The basic pose recommended for this area is Vrkasana (Tree). If you do not practice Hatha Yoga look for the recommended pose in the area provided for it (see page 274).

TAROT

Take the 22 Major Arkana cards. Choose one of the recommended spreads and observe the card that Tarot shows you. This is the archetype that helps you to work on this area. Look for the meaning of this card in the section provided for it (see pages 176-256). After looking up the definition write in your journal the meaning this card has for you at this moment.

MEDITATIVE COACHING

1. What is my purpose in life?
2. How passionate am I about what I do?
3. How do I feel about what I do?
4. What is my definition of profession and work?
5. What I am doing (the profession I practice or the work I do) how well is it working for me?
6. How much joyful effort am I willing to make to work in what I love?
7. What am I doing that works well? How can I repeat it?
8. How much enthusiasm do I feel for what I do?
9. How important is the profession I chose for me?
10. How authentic am I in my work/profession?

MEDITATIVE WRITING (THE JOURNAL)

Write down any image, sound, color or sensation you experienced during meditation. In case an image has come up, try to design it or get a photo or print showing it.

Write down the answers to the Meditative Coaching questions and reflect about each of them.

VISUALIZATION

Lie down comfortably, make sure not to be interrupted. Enter into deep relaxation through conscious breathing you practiced in meditation. Visualize yourself already practicing the profession/job you love. Feel the emotion of knowing that you do something you really like. If you want to be a doctor, visualize yourself attending your patients lovingly, and imagine seeing an expression of wellbeing and health in their faces after a visit at your office. Look at all the details, colors, smells and thank the Universe because everything is already accomplished.

Visualize yourself earning a lot of money (define what a lot of money is for you and put an amount, maybe $10,000 a month or more) feel the emotion of creating that energy.

AFFIRMATIONS

Remember that each affirmation has to be accompanied by the feeling of joy that you get when you know what your purpose is.

- I feel accomplished with the work I am doing.
- I am happy because I love what I do.
- I am blessing for everybody to whom I give service.
- My profession gives me more than enough money to do all I like.

- I am at the perfect place and time for me and everybody surrounding me.
- All my experiences are opportunities to grow.

ACTION

Set aside some time (at least one hour), meditate before you start to write about your purpose in life. What do you want to achieve? What would you like your profession to be? How can you benefit others? Author and lecturer Jack Canfield says in his book *The Success Principles,* that when you know what your purpose in life is, the world benefits too because "when you work aligned with your true purpose in life, you automatically serve others."

Recommended reading:

The Success Principles	Jack Canfield
The Master Key System	Charles Haanel
The Answer	John Assaraf
The Life You Were Born to Live	Dan Millman
Way of the Peaceful Warrior	Dan Millman

Work / Profession

I love what I do, I enjoy serving.

When I was little, I dreamt of being a

rich and famous

doctor, singer, dancer.

Only to know that what I

really wanted

was to undertake the act of

serving others.

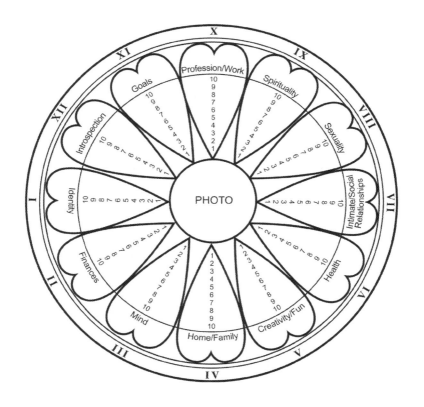

AREA XI
GOALS

Area XI

GOALS

We have heard the word "goal" many times. However there are people who do not know what it means. For some a goal is an objective, while others use both words as if they were synonymous.

Some people set a goal for themselves, they set their objectives and use one or several strategies to reach them and achieve that goal.

In the context of this book when we talk about goals we refer to whatever you want to achieve and manifest. It can be buying your first home, a car, have a united and happy family or the job you always wanted, among other things. The objectives are the steps which make it possible for you to comply with this goal. For example: if your goal is buying a home, your objective could be keeping a good credit rate and the strategy (action plan) could be opening a savings account that helps you make it come true.

On the other hand, there are people who describe it in a different way, where the objective is the target to be reached and the goals are the little steps to get there. Anyway, the important thing is that you know well what you want to achieve in your life.

Having a life without goals is like getting on a plane that does not have a route or a destination to reach (remember that for this book the goals are the final destination you want to reach, the objectives are like the flight plan, and strategy is the way how you are going to reach that final destination). When you decide what you want to achieve, the energy of this decision will open the doors for you, clear the way and present people and opportunities to you to make your desires come true.

Now, do you know what you want? What is your true aspiration in life? Do you know what you want to achieve in the next three months or in the next five years?

There are people for whom it is very easy to answer these questions. However to other people it seems a frightening challenge. They do not know what they want, but at least they are sure about what they do not want to experience in their lives. This is a good starting point. If you know what you do not want, you might be interested in the opposite of that. If you do not want your car anymore, maybe you want a new one or a motor cycle. If your present job does not satisfy you anymore, maybe you want a new job where you can achieve professionalism in the field of work you chose. It is important to mention that it is not convenient for you to put your energy and attention into something you do not want. When we do that - unknowingly - we attract what we do not want.

Quantum physics (a branch of science that studies the subatomic world) states that like attracts like. If we are constantly repeating and complaining about not being satisfied with our life, we are going to attract more of the same. That is why you need to look for techniques that can help you to get out of this negative "spell" you are in.

Breathing is a good tactic. When you notice that you are thinking the same thing over and over, breathe and change your focus. Think of something pleasant and enjoy this high vibration moment. That is the way to attract enjoyable situations to your life. Another technique you could use is clapping your hands as if you were applauding. The sound gets you out of the trance you are in and immediately you can visualize what you want to bring to manifestation. Energy will move to where you put your attention and when you focus on something, it expands.

We are always hearing talks about Energy. *"She has good energy,"* *"He feels very energetic,"* *"The energy you feel here is very good,"* etc. In all the book you read about concepts like "energy" and "high energy vibration." However….do we know what energy is? What is it made of? Energy is what allows that the planets move in the Universe and that everything is vibrating: life, light, an electric current or the sound of the wind. The Energy Conservation Law says that it does not get lost or destroyed but it transforms itself. Energy is what moves, unites and sustains and everything is made of it.

The new scientists proved that apart from chemical reactions we are an energy field which in the metaphysics' world is called aura. Human beings are connected with the Universe through energy (uni= one). We are one and we are made of atoms, molecules and cells, but at the same time we act in an independent way because we have different experiences and ways of seeing life.

Our body is made of cells, formed by molecules which in turn are made of atoms. The atom is made of protons, neutrons and electrons, etc. That is why in Buddhism it is said that nothing exits in and of itself and that the world in its most basic way coexists like a complex spider web of interdependent relations (mutual dependence). We are all mutually inter-dependent.

Some scientists suggest that it is we (our state of conscientiousness) who have the key to life and even to reality. In 1967, the German engineer Konrad Zuse, who is considered the inventor of the first electronic digital computer, suggested that the Universe works like a big conscientious computer and that, as computers transform information entries into results, our cosmic consciousness seems to do the same. If we can convert information into results, we have to make sure that this information is the most appropriate one and helps us to obtain the desired results. As it is said in the computing field: *garbage in, garbage out.* That means, if you enter low energy vibration thoughts like fear, you will have the result of challenging situations that activate feelings of doubt, rancor or fury and you will remain in the same vicious cycle.

Also a series of scientific discoveries is changing our way of looking at life and everything that surrounds us. It is said that atoms, particles or waves react to the way they are observed. There is ample scientific evidence that energy reacts to our thoughts and observation. In 1998 scientists of the Weitzman Institute of Science in Israel documented this phenomenon, demonstrating that *"the more observation, the greater the influence of the observer on the final manifestation."*

More than 2.500 years ago Shakyamuni Buddha said that everything is in the mind. Today the new scientists investigate the influence we have over what we observe. Imagine what we can achieve with our mind! You are the architect of your life. With your thoughts and actions you build your future in the present and you can make your goals manifest in the physical world.

At the "I can do it" workshops I had the opportunity to hear the American author Gregg Braden speak about how our feelings help us to communicate with that Superior Energy or what many call the Universe. He explained that emotions originate from three chakras in the lower part of the body and that thoughts (logical process) occur in chakras 5, 6 and 7 in the upper part. He also said that thoughts and emotions unite in the heart to create feelings. He also emphasized that feelings are the union of thought and emotion. Braden added that emotion is energy in ***motion*** (movement). He also told us that there are two primary emotions: love and its opposite - fear. From love emerge enjoyment and happiness... and from fear hate, sadness, depression and rage among other feelings.

In the book *Ask and it is Given,* by Esther and Jerry Hicks a guideline is provided regarding the feelings with the highest energy vibration, through which we can communicate with the Universe to ask what we long for and manifest what we want to achieve.

Amanda came to me referred by one of my clients. When she filled out the Mandala for Transformation she circled number three in the Area of Goals and it was very difficult for her to answer the Meditative Coaching questions. After several meditation and visualization exercises she could see what she really wanted to achieve in her life. She became aware that she could have more than one goal.

I even told her that the most recommended thing would be to set a goal for each area and later to review the Mandala. If she wanted, she could set more than one goal in the areas she wanted. When she understood what Energy was and how it works, it was very easy for her to visualize her goals. She read all the books I recommended to her and she did all her assignments, including writing down in her journal the goals she wanted to achieve in each area, the objectives to reach them and which strategies she would use to achieve the goal she had set for herself. She made sure that her objectives were S.M.A.R.T. (Specific, Measurable, Attainable, Reasonable, Time Oriented).

When she wrote down her objectives in the journal – which she called her machine to make dreams come true – she was very specific about what she wanted to achieve. Every two weeks she checked on what level of the Mandala she was (she made one for each objective). She made sure that they were attainable (she did not want to dream about "flying birds"). She understood that the goals were reasonable because they did not create false hopes and she made sure that she could reach them in the planned timeframe.

She was very enthusiastic and worked very diligently, like a little ant. She consistently did the recommended things. She did not miss any of her appointments and worked happily on her change. She dedicated a special joyful effort to Yoga poses because she discovered that they increased her energy a lot and when she finished doing them it was easier to sit down to visualize and write her affirmations in her "Machine to make Dreams come true."

In the process of her inner work she received a great job offer outside of Puerto Rico with triple salary. Her fiancé decided to accompany her and both worked out a plan for him to get the job he desired.

One of the instruments they used was meditation. It is a way of relaxing and listening to what the Universe (God, your Superior Being, etc.) gently has to tell us. Compassion is the feeling that connects the whole Universe, and they left with hearts full of compassion and joy, which has helped them live everything they wanted so much.

MEDITATION

This meditation takes at least 20 minutes. Make sure not to be interrupted. Look for a quiet place and disconnect all the telephones. Lie down in Savasana (relaxed pose – page 269) and close your eyes. Start a conscious breathing process. When you inhale, put your attention on the first three chakras (pubis, under the navel and on the solar plexus). Observe your emotions. Breathe deeply and when you exhale put your attention on the superior chakras (throat, brow and crown). Observe your emotions. If you hear your ego sabotage you with comments like: "this is not going to work, what are you doing, this is ridiculous," breathe deeply and do not enter into the dialogue; only get back to breathing and start again. Remember that you can choose. You do not need to think that what you do is not going to work. Breathe deeply and focus on the heart. Deliberately choose to feel love and compassion. When you think the moment is right, open your eyes little by little and look at everything around you. Observe and enjoy.

YOGA

The recommended pose for this area is Virabhadrasana II (The Warrior II – page 276). Always remember to warm up your body before starting the poses routine. My recommendation is to do two or three rounds of Sun Salutation (any of the series) and then integrate the pose. Hold the pose for at least one minute and repeat it three times. Listen to your body. If you are not a Hatha Yoga Practitioner, always remember to sit down comfortably on a chair or on the floor. You have to be comfortable in the pose you have chosen in order to increase energy before you continue the process.

TAROT

Get the 22 Major Arcana cards. Choose one of the recommended spreads and observe which card the Tarot shows you. This is the archetype that will help you to work on this area. Look for the meaning of the card in the section provided for it (see pages 176-256). After looking up the definition, write in your journal the meaning that this card has for you at this moment.

MEDITATIVE COACHING

1. What is it I want to achieve?
2. In how much time do I want to achieve it?
3. Why and for what purpose do I want to do it?
4. What Action Plan do I have to accomplish it?
5. How hard am I willing to work for it?
6. What motivates me to reach my objectives?
7. How will I feel when I achieve it?
8. Now that I reached my objectives, what will stop me from reaching my goals?
9. How can I transcend what is keeping me from it?
10. When I achieve my goals, how am I going to celebrate it? How am I going to help others?

MEDITATIVE WRITING (THE JOURNAL)

Write down any image, sound, color or sensation you experienced during meditation.

Write the answers to Meditative Coaching and reflect about each of them.

AFFIRMATIONS OF GRATITUDE

Remember that any AFFIRMATION of gratitude has to be accompanied by a feeling of joy that you get when you have achieved what you wanted.

- Thank you Universe because I achieved _____
- Thank you Protective Forces of the Beloved Universe because my business is prosperous and it helps to improve all my clients' quality of life.
- Thank you God (Goddess) because I have a savings account of more than _____ (put the amount you want, the Universe is unlimited).
- Thank you God (Goddess) for the success I have achieved in all aspects of my life. I rejoice and give thanks.

VISUALIZATION (Extend love)

Lie down comfortably and make sure that there are no interruptions. Enter into a state of deep relaxation through conscious breathing which you practiced in meditation. Visualize how your thoughts (three superior chakras) harmonize and unite with your feelings (three inferior chakras) in your heart. Feel how your heart irradiates love, peace, happiness, harmony, joy and compassion. When you feel that you are filled with these high energy vibration feelings, open your eyes slowly and give thanks for being here and now building the future.

ACTION

If you do not know your goals, answer the questions of Meditative Coaching and write them down in your journal. If you have set your goals - objectives – already, enter them in your journal by areas. For 12 days (one day for each goal – or the time you decide-) observe your goals and ask yourself which small big step you can take to achieve what you have planned. Do something every day that makes you get closer to you aim, be it saving, taking your resume to an employment agency, going to a temple or church you like and praying with the intention to infuse energy into your purposes in life.

Recommended reading:

The Divine Matrix	Gregg Braden
The Field	Lynne Mc. Taggart
The Dancing Wu Li Masters	Gary Zukav
The Biology of Belief	Bruce Lipton

Goals

My dear goals

were my best

teachers in the art of letting go.

I see them, I affirm them and then

without being attached to the result,

I let go of them, with the conviction

that all of them manifest themselves

in my life.

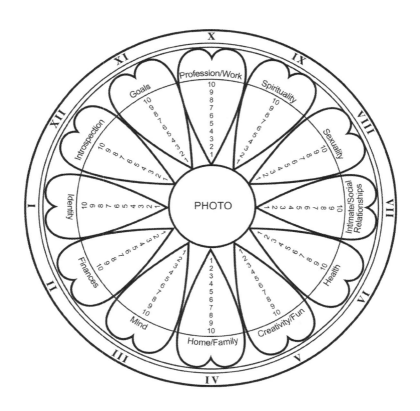

AREA XII
INTROSPECTION

Area XII

INTROSPECTION

We human beings are all good by nature. We all have the potential of illumination within us. However according to Tibetan Buddhism, the six basic deceits of the mind: attachment, anger, pride, ignorance, doubt and afflictive vision (thinking that everything exists inherently), sometimes make us act in an inappropriate way. Apart from that, if we add childhood experiences of pain (mistreatment, physical and emotional pain, violation, verbal abuse, etc.) and we do not have the necessary instruments to act correctly, we can become our worst enemy and life can become hell.

After sexual molestation, violation, humiliation and mistreatment, pain and despair will turn into anger and hate. People try to bury these experiences, and most of the time the suffering is not remembered.

If the abuse, violation and mistreatment took place during childhood, it is necessary to understand that a child does not know what is happening. He/She only feels pain and disorientation without knowing where to go or with whom to speak because the aggressor has a certain control over him/her. When the person matures and develops awareness, it is absolutely necessary to deal with these feelings and not bury or hide them, because sooner or later they will emerge. In many cases they come up like an explosion and in others like a chronic depression, and this is a reason to think that there is a disconnection from Divinity's unconditional love.

The truth frees us. It is necessary to get the help of a health professional, get the "skeletons" out of the closet and come face to face with the phantasms of the past in order to heal the pain and desperation.

Anger is one of the lowest frequency emotions and it has attacked humanity for centuries. This rage and fury can be a habit formed in childhood. Children copy and model their irate behavior from their parents, many times looking for approval, acknowledgement and love. Recognizing our past conditioning and our habits gives us the opportunity to reprogram our mind now as adults.

Some things we can do to deal with anger are: observe our rage and see what causes it, train in the virtue of patience (our spiritual practice and being compassionate is the best tool to train in this virtue). A way of getting out of fury is understanding the needs of the people who (according to our perception) caused our ire, and asking ourselves if these people are happy or if they are going through a challenge in their lives.

Other ways to work with ire are: accepting constructive criticism, admit our mistakes, learn from the people who criticize us, abandon the situation, learn from and appreciate others and allow them to express their opinion. Even if we do not agree, respecting the position of others gives us a sensation of peace because we get rid of the heavy load of ire.

What can also help us in transmuting ire is accepting our responsibility and not blame others for the situation; admit that we always have the power of decision and that we can choose to be patient and rejoice.. We have to let go of resentment, forgive others and ourselves; cultivate love for ourselves and for others are also ways to exchange ire for the high energy of compassion.

Many times we read in the newspapers about events that shock us, like murders and sexual abuse of a pregnant women or of children. The first reaction is indignation and anger, and then judgment. We immediately judge the person who committed this monstrosity and we don't stop to think what made him/her react that way. Maybe if we took some time to ask ourselves and analyze what motivated the assassin or aggressor to act the way he/she did, maybe we can see a person full of fears who probably was abused during childhood and emotionally destroyed.

That is why it is necessary to travel inside ourselves to examine our mental states, which can range from the highest to the lowest energy vibrations. When we admit and accept that we harbor low frequency feelings we want to change, we can look for the help we need. Admitting and accepting that inside ourselves there is light and darkness is the first step to be free.

If we do not do this introspection regularly, life or our karma confronts us with events and circumstances that force us to do it. It is imperative to evaluate where we stand, what we have done and which type of behavior we want to change. If we acted in a way we consider inappropriate, it is inevitable to travel inside ourselves and ponder the motives, causes and conditions that made us act this or that way. Generally, when we feel bad about ourselves (it is always important to pay attention to our feelings), sometimes it is due to the fact that we acted against our values and what we feel is right. We have to try to identify the reasons why we acted against our wellbeing, and then we have to take action to work on what we want to change. It is necessary to go on this internal journey with a heart full of compassionate love, without shame, guilt or judgments.

The best way to do it is meditating and with the Meditative Coaching. When we ask ourselves open and positive questions, the mind pauses looking for an answer. This makes us get out of the spell the mind could be under. In order to achieve this, it is necessary that you make this journey every day. If that is not possible, at least once a week you should travel inside yourself and see what is going on.

At this moment I invite you to stop everything, get your journal and start the journey.

Meditate at least 20 minutes. Then answer the following questions:

Identity:	What makes me act against who I am?
Finances:	What do I have to do to improve my relationship with money?
Mind:	What mental state made me act this way? (Fear, ire or attachment can be some of these mental states).
Home/Family	What kind of action plan can I implement to improve the relationship with my family?
Creativity/Fun:	What am I going to do to have fun and increase my creativity?
Health:	How am I going to take care of my body, mind and spirit?
Relationships:	How am I going to improve my intimate and social relations?
Sexuality:	What do I have to change to improve my sexuality?
Spirituality:	How many times a day or during the week am I in communication with my Superior Being?
Work/Profession:	How am I going to work on my attitude towards the work I am doing at the moment?
Goals:	What goals have I set for myself and how am I going to make them come true?
Introspection:	How many times a week or a month do I plan the journey inside Myself? How willing am I to observe my dark side, and what am I willing to do to work on the change lovingly?

MEDITATION

Sit down comfortably and close your eyes. Inhale deeply, continue inhaling and exhaling and if a thought comes up, slowly focus again on breathing. Continue inhaling and exhaling until you reach a state of deep relaxation. Observe your mind, if there is a thought of shame or guilt, slowly and lovingly return your attention to breathing.

Continue inhaling and when you exhale, think: I forgive myself anything I might have done in an unconscious state. Inhale and feel the freedom forgiveness brings you.

YOGA

The recommended posture for this area is Child's Pose (see page 278). When you are in this pose, surrender to the Universe and feel the calm and peace of letting go of all the burden inside you.

TAROT

Get the cards and meditate for a moment. Close your eyes and ask your inner wisdom to manifest itself through the Tarot and give you the message you need for this area (see pages 176-256).

MEDITATIVE COACHING

1. Which fears prevent me from seeing myself as I really am? A being of light!
2. What am I hiding when I act in an unconscious state?
3. Why do I feel shame?
4. What prevents me from accepting myself the way I am?
5. What prevents me from taking action to change?

MEDITATIVE WRITING (THE JOURNAL)

Write down any emotion you felt during meditation, any color or smell. Write what you felt and analyze the answers of Meditative Coaching.

AFFIRMATIONS

- I am always relaxed, I am a being of light and I live authentically.
- I accept my darkness with compassionate love and I am willing to always live in light.
- I love and accept myself the way I am.
- I am willing to change what is not beneficial for me anymore.
- I love myself with the unconditional love of the Universe.

VISUALIZATION

Lie down comfortably in Savasana (resting pose – page 269). Close your eyes and breathe deeply. Inhale and exhale until you enter a relaxed state. Visualize traveling within yourself. Observe your mind, your thoughts and your body. Pay attention to your interior dialogue, but do not enter into a conversation. Visualize those aspects as if they were little animals. Which animal would you use to describe your anger, your fear? Give them a name; for example a thought of anger could be a Tiger. Now put them all in front of you and fill them with light. Call each one by the name you gave them and thank them for being useful at certain moments, but let them know that you do not need them anymore. Say good by and let them go.

Continue inhaling and exhaling and when you consider it convenient, open your eyes slowly.

ACTION

During this week put your attention on your acts. If anything happens that does not agree with your values, analyze it and bring it to the light of your loving kindness with the purpose of changing and never doing it again.

Recommended reading:

The Dark Side of the Light Chasers   Debbie Ford
Why Good People Do Bad Things   Debbie Ford
Practicing the Path   Yangsi Rinpoche
On Being Human   Daisaku Ikeda

Introspection

When I travel inside myself

sometimes I am afraid to

see myself the way I am.

I do not want to see my dark side,

but one day I understood that

I had to bring the traits

of my darkness to light,

because it is the only way to live

happily and in peace

Ever after

TAROT

Brief analysis of the 22 Major Arcana symbolisms for the 12 Areas of the Mandala for Transformation

THE FOOL
New beginnings/Transcendental

Generally speaking, this card can mean some kind of confusion and also new beginnings. Maybe you are in a transcendental situation in your life, but it is necessary to know that there are no bad situations, all of them are caused by changes. Sometimes we perceive certain events in our lives as something bad; however they could be decisive and challenging moments which we do not necessarily label good or bad. For me something we consider a problem reveals itself over time as a blessing and benefit. Sometimes we do not see it that way, but when it happens we can recognize it and be thankful for it.

When The Fool comes up in the spread it can represent someone who wants to leave everything behind and start anew. However it can also mean that we go on our journey joyfully, without mental poison, free of attachments and ties. You will know through meditation which of the two circumstances is the one that most closely resembles what is happening at this stage of your life.

You have to focus your attention on the area from which this card comes up, because it could be that you are at a transcendental moment in this aspect of your life. The Fool could mean beginning and end. Whenever something ends, there is a new beginning.

If this card comes up in the area of:

Identity: It can symbolize that you need to know yourself and understand who you are. It is the moment of surrendering everything to Divinity and work on yourself. It is crucial for you to enter the reevaluation of your values process and to go inside yourself to discover who you are.

Finances: It is a time to observe how you invest your money. It can indicate that there is some confusion regarding the best way to do so. It is recommended that you make a budget and stick to it. This is a great opportunity to start saving and looking for the help of a financial advisor.

Mind: At this moment you could be in a state of daze and confusion. It is possible that what Buddhists call "deceptions and venoms of the mind" like ire, doubt, ignorance, attachment, pride come up. To work on these deceptions it is good to develop antidotes against them.

Ire: Use patience

Doubt: Apply logic and reason

Ignorance: Cultivate wisdom

Attachment: Practice generosity

Pride: Develop humility

Shakamuni Buda taught that life is a constant change. This precept shows us that nothing is forever, and when the undisciplined mind makes us think that nothing changes, deceptions arise that take us to pain and suffering.

Home/Family: It can convey the message that you have to start from zero. It is recommended that the whole family has a meeting and each member contributes to new agreements of living together. When they participate in making these commitments, they will feel more comfortable with them and it will also be easier to follow them. If this does not produce the expected results, look for professional help so that everybody can receive attention and the conflicts they are going through can be resolved.

Creativity/Fun: You need to look for new ways of having fun and revive your creativity. Make an appointment with and for yourself and comply with it. Sit down and meditate for awhile and ask yourself: "What do I like?" Go bowling, to the beauty spa, look at a flower, go to the beach ? ......Whatever it is, it is important for you to do something that gives you pleasure and enjoyment at least once a week.

You can also unleash your creativity on canvas. Paint without judging yourself, only let go of what manifests itself through your hands and have fun doing so. Admire your work and put it at a visible place so that when you look at it you remember that you are a Creator.

Health: Fast action is recommended in this area. You have to see a health professional and do all the necessary analyses. The body is the airplane that takes us on our journey and we have to give it the necessary maintenance. This card tells you to take care of your health immediately.

Relationships: It is necessary to review the agreements of the relationship. It is essential to make time to cultivate it. In case you have to start from the beginning, set the rules to do so. Relationships are like plants, you have to water and love them so they can bloom. If after having done everything for the relationship to continue you do not achieve the desired success, it is the moment to release, let go and start again.

Sexuality: It could mean that this is the moment to analyze the relationship with your partner regarding sexuality. If you do not have a partner, look for a healthy way to manage sexual energy. If you have any kind of dissatisfaction or doubt in this aspect, get professional help.

Spirituality: It is a call for mysticism and the *common union* with God. It is necessary to let go of old believes and be like children before God.

Profession: It is a good time to reevaluate what you are doing. Reflect, prepare an action plan and act it out.

Goals: It is possible that you are a little confused. This is a good moment to analyze, reflect and look inside yourself. Meditate and use all the instruments provided in this book so you can set new goals for yourself. Every day is a new beginning and wise people start anew.

Introspection: You are asked to look inside yourself. During this journey it is necessary to let go of old believes. You have to start the trip full of confidence and with a happy and adventurous heart. Only you know if at this moment your journey is happy and fun. Trust that something good is going to manifest itself in your life. Introspection is one of the areas with most analysis. It will take you to the depth of your being in order to emerge victoriously to the surface.

I

THE MAGICIAN
Transmutation/Positive

This card may symbolize performing a responsibility which satisfies us, it could be on an emotional, material or spiritual level. The Magician is the alchemist, the one who helps us change the challenges that present themselves in our life. It indicates that we have the desire and capacity to act. It symbolizes words, creativity and actions we are able to do to achieve the goals we have set out for ourselves. It represents our capacity and interest in resolving challenging situations.

In any area this card appears, it represents the originality we already have to use the energy of Transmutation (transformation we are creating little by little on our way to self realization) and achieve what we aspire to. We have to use this power of Transmutation wisely and with common sense to do good to others. These energies should never be directed at harming anybody, because any kind of energy we send out will come back to us multifold.

The Magician means that we have to put our soul into what we do. It is a call to action to concentrate all our attention and interest on making what we yearn for come true.

If this card comes up in the area of :

Identity: It symbolizes that it is the moment to act. You have to take the necessary steps to know who you are and what your purpose in life is.

Finances: It can indicate that you need wisdom to invest money energy. It is possible that you have a safe source of income like a fixed salary, but maybe it is not a big amount. However the appearance of this card indicates that if you are willing to invest time, energy and knowledge, you can make your finances reach the desired level.

Mind: It represents the need for you to analyze all you are going to do, use tenacity and common sense in your plans to achieve the goals you set for yourself. It can indicate that you are a little obstinate and that you have not yet considered all the possible alternatives you might have to resolve a situation. It also symbolizes your analytical capacity and the energy that helps you to solve all the situations you are going through. The message it sends is that you can transmute what you want.

Home/Family: It indicates that we must have loving details with our partner and more compassion. It is necessary to put emotion into the relationship. It can also show us to act and motivate our children so they learn to pursue and achieve their dreams.

Apart from that it can reveal to us that we are not happy with the place we live in and that maybe it would be good to make some changes to improve it.

Creativity/Fun: Your energy is "potentializing" itself to be used correctly and bring every-thing you imagined to manifestation.

The Magician means originality and creativity and tells us to act on them. It also indicates that we have to take time out to have fun and put our heart into what we enjoy.

Health: It lets us know that a medical evaluation is necessary. It is important to see the doctor we trust and have all the necessary tests done. This body is the airplane that takes us where we want to go, therefore you have to give it maintenance to guarantee optimum performance. Specially focus on the throat, thyroid, larynx and neck problems.

Relationships: It shows our capacity to influence other people, which has to be guided by love and compassion. As in sexuality, it is necessary to put imagination, creativity and fun in our relationships to make them happy and enjoyable.

Sexuality: Now is the moment to act. It is necessary to add imagination, creativity and fun to the sexual relation with our partner. It is time to explore new alternatives that ignite it and make you enjoy a good sexual relation to the fullest. Remember however that these new practices cannot go against your values. If you do not have a partner, learn to explore your body until you reach and positively use the powerful energy of an orgasm.

Spirituality: It shows that it is necessary to unite thoughts and emotions. It is our ability to take action. Our intuition is starting to blossom. The Magician is the alchemist and transmutes (changes) everything he touches. It is a call for daily meditation.

Profession: It represents love and positive energy in what you do. It is your ability to succeed at all tasks given to you to carry out. However it could also mean that you are spending too much time on your job, and nothing on yourself and your family. If this is the case, get the Meditative Coaching questions and make an action plan to enjoy your family and yourself more.

Goals: It shows you your energy and determination to reach your goals. When The Magician comes up in this area, you have the best opportunities to make your dreams come true. Use your intuition, creativity and imagination to draw up the action plan. Write down your objectives and plan the strategy that will help you to manifest all you desire.

Introspection: It indicates that you have everything to travel inside yourself. You have the courage to look straight at yourself. You have the capacity to transmute everything you want to change in your personality.

II

THE HIGH PRIESTESS
Positive/Enriching

It is a positive card. In every area it shows it means gestation, receptivity and germination. It is something that enters your life without you noticing it and takes root silently but firmly. Experiences are what form your character. For example: the first money you earned on your job. Do you remember the feeling of joy you had? There are moments in our existence that serve as steps to go up to a better way of seeing life. Get your journal and write down those moments for you.

The High Priestess is the protector of wisdom, she is the woman who has matured in time. She has internalized the teachings of life and is happy to have done so. She represents the possibility of self realization, the immutable persistence that pushes you to achieve your goals. It is the stability you get from experience. The High Priestess is the teacher who lives what she preaches and from whom you can learn everything.

When The High Priestess reveals herself in any of the areas, she represents the link between something that has not manifested itself (what we cannot see yet) and the manifested things (what has already materialized in our lives). She is intuition with the highest energy vibration to help us to materialize what we have worked on with perseverance.

If this card comes up in the area of:

Identity: It indicates to you that your intuition is the greatest instrument you have to achieve all your goals. It reveals that you have an innate wisdom, given to you the day you were born. Now you only have to put your power into action.

Finances: It is a call for patience, because this virtue will make you triumph. One of the goals you can establish for yourself is to have a reserve fund. In order to do this you have to save, even if it is only $5.00 a week. Any amount is good when you have the intention to accomplish it. This card represents the germination of all your efforts to achieve financial peace. Make sure your wishes are clear, conscientious and for the good of all.

Mind: It indicates that you have to unify your knowledge, your common sense and your capacity of reflection on an intellectual level in order to take care of the situations in your life at this moment. It is necessary for you to meditate daily to activate your wisdom and act with serenity to face the challenges you confront.

Home/Family: It shows a home where love, patience and perseverance have to be invested. Love is the force that moves, unites and forgives everything. It is important for you to use your discernment and sensibility to achieve the family union you long for.

Creativity/Fun: It notifies you that you need immediate attention in this area. Maybe you dedicate all your time to others and have forgotten yourself. Answer the following questions: "Do I make enough time for myself? How many times a week do I have at least one hour to do what I like and is fun; or just to stay in silence?" If that is not the case, create your personal agenda and make an appointment with yourself and keep it.

Health: It can indicate that it is necessary to see your gynecologist and do all the tests regarding your sex- and reproductive organs. The Priestess symbolizes our feminine organs: breasts, ovaries, matrix. It can also mean fertility, and that is why it is convenient to have a pregnancy test done.

Relationships: It could be a sign that it is necessary to be cautious in this area. It could indicate that you are giving up your power to please others. The High Priestess is a selfless woman or man, totally immersed in their relationships, be it with friends, at work or a romantic involvement. They tend to please others, forgetting about themselves and what truly makes them happy.

Sexuality: Your sexual relation is probably evolving into a quieter, more passive and satisfactory one. The appearance of The Priestess notifies you that you have to take your partner's desires into consideration and also your point of view regarding the issue. Both of you have to be satisfied with the relation, if not, it is necessary to look for the help of a health professional who will guide you so you can achieve harmony.

Spirituality: It can reveal that your intuition is on a very high energy point. It is the moment to attract new opportunities to your life that will help you to make your dreams come true. Your intuition will take you on new paths which you can explore at this moment of gestation. This energy will liberate itself little by little. Visualize the result of your desire and give thanks as if you were experiencing it.

Profession: It is a good moment for new projects that will emerge little by little. Everything you take on can have a happy accomplishment. It is recommended to be discrete with what you are planning.

Goals: Due to the fact that The Priestess is a positive card it can be the happy ending for the accomplishment of all your desires. It can also mean the wellbeing you will feel upon reaching your goals. It also shows us that it is necessary to have patience and work little by little to manifest what we long for.

Introspection: It can mean here that this is a moment for meditation, reflection and silence. Use the *Meditative Coaching* questions and reconsider your answers. Remain objective and take the necessary action to change what has to be renewed in your life.

III

THE EMPRESS
Positive/Promising

The Empress represents the dedication and efficiency of feminine energy, know as Yin in the Orient. She is a woman irradiating power and determination. She is intelligent, capable of recognizing and using her talents. She knows how to effectively manage the resources of others to achieve her objectives. She is aware of new strategies that help her to reach her goals. She is the woman who knows how to make correct decisions that take her to make her wishes come true. If you are a man, this card shows your feminine energy which you have to use in an efficient way to achieve your goals. The Empress confirms that you have the capacity to create a life full of love and financial prosperity.

In all the areas the card comes up it can indicate success, evolution, progress and stability. It offers a promising future.

If this card comes up in the area of:

Identity:
It means that it is vital to use The Empress' energy. It is a good moment to define your identity and to recognize the power within you. Intelligence and capacity to set goals and make plans for the future are attributes you have to mange in your favor.

Finances:
It can indicate that what you are going to undertake will be successful. Take advantage of this energy to put your savings plan into action. You can get a good offer to manage your money at the bank of your preference. Look for information on how to maximize the money you have and analyze it before taking action.

Mind:
It informs you that it is necessary to get in touch with your feelings. Look into your heart for the answers to your questions. It always has the true answers. Learn to trust your feelings more.

Home/Family:
It is an alert to take the events happening at home more seriously. The ruling authority has to be one of love and compassion. Be truthful with your family; express what you feel, taking into consideration the feeling of the others. If something you do not agree with has happened, express what you want with love and use your power of persuasion with sweetness in order to bring the situation to a happy ending.

Creativity/Fun: It suggests that you can be very original in order to activate Creativity and Fun in your life. It cautions however that it is necessary for you to practice it. Maybe you dedicate too much time to your work and other social tasks, risking quality time you could spend with your family and yourself. As well as for the Priestess,

> you have to answer the following questions: "Do I make enough time for myself? How many times a week do I have at least one hour to do what I like and what is fun; or simply to spend it in silence ?" If you do not have that, get your personal agenda, make an appointment with yourself and keep it. You can find peace in nature. Walking in the countryside or along the beach could be right for you at this moment.

Health: It reveals to us that we have to put special attention on the throat, trachea and vocal chords. If you have a health challenge in one of these areas, see the doctor you trust. It also signals to us that we have to work with our fifth chakra (located in the throat). It can represent anything we have not told for fear of hurting others. Communicate with your body and try to feel what it wants or needs.

Relationships: It can be that you have not been very tolerant. It is necessary that you use your talent to show more compassion for the people around you. Get rid of the need to be flattered and show more interest in the situations and problems of others. It is a call for empathy.

Sexuality: It indicates that it is imperative to satisfy your erotic needs. You have to act with your heart and not with your head. Sexuality is not a business you have to run, it is the best and biggest association you can make. It is a call for you to put love and affection in what you want to express so that you can feel pleasure in the sexual relation.

Spirituality: It can mean that your intuition is trying to communicate something to you. It is important that you synchronize with your Superior Being in order to see which course of action to take.

Profession: It could be the moment when you get some appreciation for your work. It is recommended that you use your talent, your leadership and power of attraction to get the best out of others. The appearance of The Empress in this area signals that it is a good time to be part of a cause that helps the less fortunate.

Goals: It could indicate that the goals you have set for yourself are going to manifest themselves little by little. You will have some benefit because you worked on your objectives joyfully.

Introspection: This is the moment to go within yourself and get in touch with your feelings. You are at a perfect moment to reposition yourself and try to get a balance between your emotions and your intellect.

IV

THE EMPEROR

Positive/Promising

In the kingdom of The Emperor you will feel a consciousness of order and expansion. Sometimes it shows a person that can be irreverent, but most of the time it represents those who want and can help. The appearance of this figure in a spread can be a confirmation of the Divinity's help that arrives even if we do not expect it. It symbolizes generosity, spontaneous or providential benefits. It is logic and reason, versus love and comprehension. Sometimes this card reminds us that we have to be careful with the desire to control everything because it can be an impediment in achieving what we wish.

It personifies the leader, power, authority and discipline. In any area it shows up it can mean that the challenging situations that arise will be easily resolved.

If The Emperor comes up in the area of:

Identity: It can indicate that we have to reevaluate our values. Maybe our ego is making us think that we are more powerful than others and that we control everything.

Finances: It indicates that everything related to our finances can be resolved well. The Emperor's positive energy together with our action will help us to manifest financial peace of mind.

Mind: It indicates that it is necessary to let go of the desire to control. The focus has to be put on the present moment and we have to understand that the only thing we can control when we meditate in a disciplined way are our thoughts and sometimes not even that.

Home/Family: It describes that it is a good moment to enjoy your home and family. It is convenient for you to find the positive side of situations happening in the family circle because there is always something to learn in anything that goes on.

Creativity/Fun: The indication is that you know what you like and how to express your creativity. The Emperor knows how to have fun. Having fun is innate in you, you like to find new ways of having a good time and you really enjoy it. However it is good to be careful and avoid any excesses.

Health: It reveals to us that it is necessary to pay special attention to the liver, feet, right ear and pancreas. It is necessary to be careful with excesses because your way of having fun could damage your health.

Relationships: Maybe you need to evaluate the bases of your relationships.

You have to pay attention to your ego power in order not to hurt the sensibility of people you relate to.

Sexuality: It means that your desire to control and your energy as a leader can make you manipulate and establish a relationship of sexual power. At this moment it is necessary to protect the relationship and to understand that two people who love each other are sharing it, and that is why no one must control the other.

Spirituality: It could symbolize the need to lock on to the Divine Energy within you. It is absolutely necessary to activate your relationship with the Divinity inside you. Use the instruments we show you in the book so you can reconnect.

Profession: It is a good moment to observe what it is you really want to do. The Emperor means recognition, help of Divinity. It is also possible that at this moment you get the help you have been waiting for in order to undertake any project you have been planning.

Goals: It teaches you that The Emperor's discipline helps you to reach your goals. If you let go of control – the desire that what you planned comes out the way you want it – the Universe will move in your favor. It is the moment to surrender everything to God. This does not imply renouncing your goals, only that you give up the desire to control everything.

Introspection: It is a call for releasing and letting go. It is the time to reflect and find out what pushes you to try to control everything that happens around you. Take advantage of this moment. The Universe protects you, trust.

V

THE HIEROPHANT
Positive/Conservative

The Hierophant is a figure who values family very much. This figure represents the dogma and everything established. It can show a person who considers moral values unbreakable.

Maybe he/she can be too traditional and clinging to the past and so it is a great challenge to adapt to the present moment. Generally he/she takes good care of his/her image and attaches importance to what other people say.

It is a positive card and when it comes up it can indicate that the results of a situation or project are going to be effective. If we use The Hierophant's structured energy and his discipline we will achieve our goals within the reasonable time we have scheduled.

If The Hierophant reveals himself in the area of:

Identity: It tells us that we absolutely have to be more flexible and not judge ourselves so severely. It is necessary to become balanced and not impose our criteria on others.

Finances: It can show that we have an excessive fixation on wasting money, be it spending too much or because of the concern not to spend excessively due to a shortage mentality. One of The Hierophant's characteristics is being a good provider for his family. Even though, this can sometimes result in unlimited expenses. One has to know how to say no to an exaggerated requirement by a family member.

Mind: It indicates to us that we have to be more flexible. It is an invitation to empty our mind and to experiment that there is more than one way to obtain the results we want.

Home/Family: It describes that this is a good moment to let go of family control. It is a call for preserving peace in the home and to learn to analyze all members' points of view.

Creativity/Fun: It teaches us that if we stop fearing what others might say, we can really enjoy ourselves, even if it is playing with water. Many times we are so subject to what others think that we forget ourselves. If you meditate you will find new and unusual ways to show your creativity and have fun. Let all the happiness inside you come out.

Health: It shows us that it is necessary to put special attention on the heart, circulation and the upper part of the back. It is always good to do all necessary medical tests and not to postpone what we know is needs to be done.

Relationships: It can mean that it is necessary to understand that our values do not have to be those of others. It is essential to learn to respect other people the way they are and appreciate their Buddhist and/ or Christic nature. When we understand that the Supreme Intelligence of the Universe is within each of us, we appreciate people the way they are without wanting to change them.

Sexuality: It suggests that it is good to learn to enjoy sexual energy. It is an invitation to become flexible in your sexual behavior and to be who you really are.

Spirituality: This is the moment to get close to God; to connect with the Divine Energy within us. It can indicate that we should not continue rating our lives according to our success, money, work or economic position. It is a call to listen to our inner voice in order to be in harmony with the mind, emotions and spirit.

Profession: It shows us that we have to learn how to work on and go along with the situations we encounter. It is recommended to look for new alternatives and not to cling to the past. When The Hierophant appears in the Profession area, it tells us that there is more than one way to achieve our goals. Open your mind and listen to your intuition.

Goals:

It means that as with The Emperor card, The Hierophant's structure and discipline help you to reach your goals in the reasonable timeframe you projected for it. Your iron will, will help you to overcome the obstacles that present themselves.

Introspection:

It is the moment to look inside and accept responsibility of what happens around you. It is the moment to permit the Divine Intelligence to enter your life. Let go of the attachments to the past. Get out of the routine, experience new things and surrender everything to Divinity. God will always guide your steps, you only have to trust.

VI

THE LOVERS
Impartial/Transient

The Lovers' card represents making decisions. It is the crossroad where we are and we do not know which way to go.

It teaches that any circumstance people go through can be transient.

Apart from this it can represent the power of love and personal commitment to achieve our goals. Analysis, reflection and meditation are necessary to make correct decisions that benefit everybody involved in the situation.

It is an impartial card. It is neither yes nor no, it only indicates that it is necessary to discern at the moment of decision making.

If The Lovers shows up in the area of:

Identity:	It indicates to us that it is vital to make some time in order to analyze who we are. There may be many doubts at the moment regarding what we want in life and what our purpose in it is.
Finances:	It can show that it is necessary to make a decision how to invest and save money. Maybe you spend more than you should. Sit down and make a savings plan you can easily comply with.
Mind:	It says that there can be some confusion. The storyteller within us (the ego) is generally not right, you do not have to believe everything you think. Meditate and separate the weed from the wheat.
Home/Family:	It can make the point that your present situation is transient. It is like a hurricane, we are worried but we know that everything will pass. Nothing is permanent. It can also be that you have thought of moving or making some changes in the decoration of your home. It is a good moment to activate the energy that could be trapped somewhere in the house. Changing furniture to another place and painting can help you move the energy.
Creativity/Fun:	It signals that Fun and Creativity are easy for you. However sometimes, due to time pressure you do not take the necessary time to enjoy what you do. It indicates that you have to make time for yourself to have fun and to do what you like. Use this moment of creativity to meditate and reflect about new projects.
Health:	It is recommended to put special attention on the respiratory system : lungs and bronchia. Also focus on the central nervous system, arms and hands.

Relationships: It could mean the beginning of new relationships. Become a member of a Yoga, Tai Chi or Meditation group. It is an excellent opportunity to serve. Look for a group where you can help. When you help others you are helping yourself to increase energetic vibrations.

Sexuality: Maybe it indicates that you like to express what you feel. Maybe it is the moment to make a decision and express to your partner what you would like to experiment in the sexual relation.

Spirituality: It is time to decide which spiritual path you are going to follow. It is a time to reevaluate your spiritual practice and see if it is the one that gives you peace, happiness and enjoyment.

Profession: It is necessary to select between what you are doing and what you really would like to do in your life. Look for the Meditative Coaching questions in the Profession area, answer them and you will have a better idea about the way to go.

Goals: It can reveal that maybe you have several goals you would like to achieve As in the Profession area, look for the Meditative Coaching questions in the Goals sector and it will be easier for you to see to which goal you will dedicate more time and energy at the moment.

Introspection: Maybe there is some kind of duality in your life. Search for the truth within yourself. Meditate, analyze and reflect about what truly gives sense to your life.

VII

THE CHARIOT
Positive/Active

The Chariot teaches us that when we take control of our thoughts everything is possible. We understand that when we observe our thoughts we can direct them to a new and better state of consciousness. The Chariot is like the mind, it is necessary to take its reins to avoid going on rampages during our life.

It also indicates that it is overcoming challenges that present themselves, it is the ability we have to design our destiny and to see further than what is apparent.

It is a positive card and it moves us to action.

When The Chariot comes up in the area of:

Identity:
It shows that you have the capacity and qualities to achieve your goals. If you are consistent, determined and patient you can make your dreams come true.

Finances:
It is the opportunity The Universe gives you to take good control of your finances, be more consistent and watch very well how you invest money. Nobody can do your work for you. You have to take the reins of your financial health, so you can go forward with the goals you have set for this area.

Mind:
It reveals to us that it is time to see what happens in our mind and what kind of thoughts we have. Are they based on fear, pain, uncertainty? Analyze all angles of a situation well. With this card in the Mind area you have every opportunity to be successful if you let go of the fears that hold you back.

Home/Family:
It can indicate that you have to take the reins of your home at this instant. You are the one that can solve what is going on. You have the capacity of analysis, emotional control and logics which are necessary to solve the conflicts your family members are going through. If after having used all your love trying to do it you do not get the expected results look for the help of a health professional.

Creativity/Fun:
It denotes that Fun and Creativity is something you have to take care of. Maybe it is a little difficult for you to have a good time without feeling guilty due to your high sense of responsibility. Let go of the guilt and have some fun. Use your creative mind to find ways of having enjoyment and fun in your life. A bitter person cannot be joyfully responsible, even if he/she wants to be.

Health: It is recommended to focus your attention on the bone system. It is a good moment to see your dentist. Be careful with your knees when you do your exercises.

Relationships: It can indicate that sometimes a certain mistrust exists which makes you want to control the relationship with friends, at work or with the family. If you manage your relationships in a tactful, diplomatic and respectful way they will be successful.

Sexuality: It indicates that it is difficult for you to show your desires. Maybe you are a little inhibited because you want to control everything in the relationship.

Spirituality: It shows that it is time to activate Divine Energy. It is the moment to give thanks for everything you have. Make a list of all the blessings God gave you and go over it every day.

Profession: It suggests that when you use your great sense of responsibility and perseverance you will triumph. Your capabilities and knowledge will help you to be successful in your profession.

Goals: It indicates that when you work responsibly and you are satisfied with it you will be successful. If you take charge of the action plan you develop for yourself you will reach your goals.

Introspection: It tells you that an analysis is necessary to see what you need to change in order to achieve everything you want in this life. It is the moment to get all the skeletons out of your closet. Work on your mind in order to make new recordings of success and abundance. It affirms life and success.

VIII

STRENGTH
Positive/Discipline/Perseverance

Strength shows us the serenity we must have when we face challenging situations. It is a call for disciplined meditation so that at moments when we think that everything is lost, we understand that there is a message unknown to us that God has for everybody. This card is a symbol of the inner strength Divinity gives us in order to go ahead.

It represents the joyful effort we have to work with in order to overcome the obstacles in reaching our goals. It means using this interior strength to get over the dark side in all of us and which can make us think that we are not able to face any challenge, because we lost our strength. It is at that moment when our survival instinct makes us stay afloat to continue fighting.

In any area this card comes up it means the determination we must have to achieve our purpose and reach our goals. It is a positive card if you use all the instruments we present to you in this book with determination.

If the Strength card shows up in the area of:

Identity:
It can indicate that you are passing challenging moments in order to know who you really are. This card invites you to see that you are a being of light with a Christic and/or Buddhist nature within you. Recognize who you are, and you can achieve success in the rest of the areas in your life.

Finances:
It suggests that you are going through a moment of financial challenges. It is time to restructure the way you invest your money. You have to control your expenses, draw up a budget and honor it so you can go ahead.

Mind:
Maybe you are passing through moments of anger. If you feel very dazed and you think that there is no way out of the situation you are living right now, it is important to look for the help of a psychologist. He or she will help you to see the motive or motives of your rage more clearly. It is convenient to analyze that generally we are angry at ourselves but that we tend to project it onto others.

Home/Family:
It is possible that you have conflicts at home. It is necessary to act with serenity. You need to use your Spiritual Force to be in harmony with all your family members. The help of a conflict mediator or family psychologist is recommended in these cases.

Creativity/Fun:
It indicates that you cannot postpone the moment you need to let go of everything that makes you angry. Having fun and using your creativity to find ways to relax are a must. It is necessary to direct all your energy into making time for yourself to enjoy yourself and be more creative.

Health: It points out the importance to take care of headaches which could be affecting you. Even if they may be transitory you should see your doctor. It can also suggest to you to take care of your red blood cells.

Relationships: It could be a call for a sincere and loyal conversation with one of the people with whom you have a relationship, it could be your partner or one of your friends. Remember that love and trust give you the opportunity to resolve any type of situation.

Sexuality: It is possible that you have a lot of difficulties with your sexual relation. Maybe it is a little brusque and you have to put more spirituality and unconditional love into it.

Spirituality: It is an indication that the light within you gives you the necessary energy to go ahead on your spiritual path. You have the strength to overcome temptations that may come up on the way.

Profession: Maybe you are going through a very challenging moment at work. If you use all your strength, discipline and determination you will see that you transcend it and emerged victoriously.

Goals: It indicates to us that this is the moment to use all our discipline and perseveration to reach our goals. Due to the fact that Strength is a positive card, it can signal that if you use you inner strength, discipline, perseverance, an unbreakable determination and self – confidence you will conquer all the obstacles that present themselves and achieve your goals.

Introspection: It can mean big struggles inside you. Remember :
patience, perseverance, strength and a lot of love
will help you to harmonize your interior dialog.
This card symbolizes the triumph of love over
anger and rancor.

IX

THE HERMIT
Transcendental/ Passive

The Hermit represents wisdom, patience, perseverance. It is understanding that, as expressed in the saying, "Time fixes everything." It is becoming aware that everything can be solved in time. It is knowing how to wait and be sure that even if it does not look like it, everything is going to resolve itself to our benefit and the one of everybody involved in the situation.

It is a card that helps us transcend any challenging situation we encounter with its energy. It indicates to us that patience is a virtue worth cultivating, because if we are patient we can obtain anything.

If The Hermit comes up in the area of:

Identity:	It reveals that sometimes you can feel a little solitary, tired or grieving. It is as if you had aged in an instant. It is a call to reflect about your life and the way you are living it. This card can sometimes mean that your responsibilities are overwhelming you to the point where you ask yourself if all this sacrifice is necessary to achieve peace and harmony.
Finances:	It invites us to be patient. When we open a savings account, many times we want to see results immediately. This card teaches us that the process can be slow but secure.
Mind:	It is possible that at this moment you feel alone and anguished. The Hermit exhorts you to make daily meditation a habit. If you practice it with patience the distractions of your mind will diminish and you can have a sensation of peace and serenity. When the mind is calm it makes joyful thoughts possible. That is how you will understand that you will never be alone. God is always with you. I recommend that every day you make the affirmation evoked by Hindu master Dada J.P.Vaswani: "I am never alone, God is always with me." Repeat it several times a day, until it is part of your life.
Home/Family:	It expresses some melancholy. Maybe you want things to be different. Communication with all the family members is essential right now. It is necessary for you to express your feelings in a loving way and that you reach agreements to shorten the apparent emotional distances that exist between you.

Creativity/Fun: It can indicate that you are locked up in yourself. It reveals a tendency of not expressing your emotions. It is as if Creativity were on hold. It is necessary to get out of your lockup and open the way to your creative thoughts. Use your imagination to express what you feel.

Health: You have to specially focus on your bones and knees. Additionally a visit to the dentist is recommended.

Relationships: It can indicate that sometimes you feel alone and anguished. This can happen because you have a tendency to turn inward. It is a good time to join a Yoga or Tai Chi group so you meet people other than those around you.

Sexuality: Here it could indicate that you feel powerless facing the situation you are living right now as a couple. It can also reveal that there is a certain dissatisfaction and it is recommended to see a sexologist together with your partner. If you do not have a partner it is a good idea to learn to know your body and use sexual energy wisely.

Spirituality: It shows that your patience is bearing the expected fruit. Meditation and the passing of time bring solutions and answers to your questions.

Profession: You could go through a moment of professional dissatisfaction. Maybe you are overwhelmed, tired and in a state of stagnation at work. You want your work and your experience to be acknowledged. Remember that when you go ahead with your action plan, success will be a question of time. Have patience.

Goals: It can reveal that it is an excellent time to review your long-term goals. Meditation is absolutely necessary to fix new dates and to think about that making your goals come true is maybe taking time, but if you put all your endeavor and discipline into it, you can do it.

Introspection: It is a good moment to be alone to meditate (see instructions in the Meditation area), and use study and reflection as tools to achieve inner wisdom. This will give you the necessary knowledge to make wise decisions.

X

THE WHEEL OF FORTUNE
Positive/ Dynamic

The Wheel of Fortune means a transformation of the way you see the situations that come up. It has to do with change and transcendence because it shows us the cycles our life goes through. According to Buddhism nothing is permanent, everything changes, everything evolves in cycles day to day, moment to moment. Clinging to people, objects and situations keeps us inside the unending wheel of pain and suffering. The Wheel of Fortune teaches us that we can evolve to a new and better life.

This card reminds us that everything passes; the only constant is change, and it talks about harmonious changes where Divinity is always in our favor. Due to the fact that the wheel is in constant movement it represents changes that can be positive for our evolution

It suggests to us that we are the ones who have to take the helm of our lives and that when we activate the wheel, an energy movement is produced that helps us to get out of the impasse where we might be.

If this card comes up in the area of:

Identity:
It indicates that you are at a moment of evolution. There are changes you have to make in order to integrate your personality into the other areas of your life. That means that your thoughts, words and actions have to be in accordance. What you think and say has to agree with what you do.

Finances:
It can mean that sometimes you are at the bottom of the wheel and other times on top. That is why sometimes money flows satisfactorily in your life but on other occasions it does not come to you the way you wish. This card indicates to you that an action plan to save and sticking to it until you reach your goals is recommended.

Mind:
It signals that you may be tied to something between your past and present which you have not been able to transcend. This card indicates to you that the moment has come to let go of what does not let you expand and prepare for a new cycle in your life. On the other hand it can be an indication for you to take the controls of your plane and start your flight.

Home/Family:
It shows a home where sometimes there is harmony and sometimes it is necessary to work on keeping it. The positive and dynamic energy of this card reveals to you that love and compassion will help you to have harmony established in your home.

Creativity/Fun: It notifies you that you may be going through moments fluctuating between joy and suffering. Sometimes you are at the bottom of the wheel and sometimes on top, but independently of where you are, it is important to dedicate time to pamper yourself and do the things you like best. That is how your energy will increase and creativity and fun will come up spontaneously.

Health: It tells us that balance is necessary. We sometimes can exaggerate our way of having fun, eat and drink. It could tell you to focus more on your liver.

Sexuality: It suggests that you analyze at which part of the Wheel of Fortune you are. When you are at the upper part, your sexual relation is joyful and fun, you enjoy it a lot and it satisfies you. On the other hand, when you are at the lower part, depressed and sad, you do not wish for anything. Analyze yourself and if you discover that you are at the lower part, take immediate action and see a sexologist.

Spirituality: It indicates that your intuition is widening. A new spiritual cycle opens up for you and your life will be evolving to a new and better state of consciousness.

Profession: It suggests that it is an auspicious moment for any project you have in mind. What you will do at this time of your life has a good possibility for success. It is also necessary to evaluate at which part of the wheel you are. If your energy is low it is recommended that you do the Yoga exercises for this area

Goals: It indicates that your goals will be achieved the way you planned it because the Wheel of Fortune is a positive card. Good planning and a solid system of believes can make you reach your goals. A belief is something on your mind which you have been repeating until you think it is true. Your system of believes are ideas or experiences you have been absorbing since you were a child. The ideas were transmitted to you by your parents, teachers, uncles and aunts, grandparents and you have been repeating them without making sure if they are true or not. You just thought they were correct because they came from an authority figure. Your experiences mark what you think today, without understanding that events will not always happen the same way.

Introspection: It can mean that you are at a good moment to analyze the situations happening in your life. It is a favorable time for the reevaluation of your system of believes, and after much analysis and meditation you will act according to what you validated as correct. Trust your capabilities and above all, believe in the Universe/God.

XI

JUSTICE
Active

Justice means balance, equilibrium. As it is said in Buddhism, it is the joyous effort we have to make to achieve our goals and make our dreams come true.

In any area this card comes up it means that there is a lot of internal work to be done.

It is necessary to go further than required and to go the extra mile.

It is the quest between inner and outer balance. It is the harmony needed to bring a situation to a happy ending.

It is considered an active card that indicates to us that it is necessary to harmonize our thoughts, emotion and actions in order to achieve what we want.

If The Justice card comes up in the area of:

Identity:
It notifies you that it is necessary to look for balance in your personal life. It reminds you that it is absolutely necessary to keep all the areas in balance in order to have a harmonious and happy life.

Finances:
It represents the balance between what you receive and what you spend. You cannot spend more money than the amount that enters your account. This card also alerts you about the importance of blessing your financial commitments. When you are going to pay your bills bless them and bless the supplier who believed in you so you could get the goods and services you are enjoying now.

Mind:
It signals the need to look for balance of your thoughts. It can indicate that you have a mental hustle and bustle that is so strong that sometimes you cannot even function properly in day to day activities. It can also notify that in severe cases you have to consult a psychologist who can help you to clarify your ideas.

Home/Family:
It expresses the search for balance in the family. It shows us that it is necessary to be fair with all family members and inform about the need to dedicate the same amount of time to all of them. It can also mean that you have to give priority to some family matter instead of your work, special activity, including even religion or politics. The sense of Justice is essential in living harmoniously and in peace with your loved ones.

Creativity/Fun: Maybe it is telling you that you are too inclined to enjoy yourself and have neglected other aspects of your life. As well as in the other areas, it is necessary to balance fun with the rest of the professional and personal responsibilities. It may indicate that Creativity is at a moment to be balanced. It is necessary to incline the balance more to this aspect. Maybe you could think of taking ceramic, painting, jewelry creating classes or anything that makes your dormant creativity come alive.

Health: You have to put special attention on your kidneys, bladder and waist. Drink a lot of water to hydrate your kidneys and keep your urinary tract in optimum conditions.

Relationships: Here it means that balance in your relationships is necessary. Observe if the balance is more inclined to please others or to please yourself.

Sexuality: It is the moment to look for balance in your sexual and love life. Sexuality without love does not make sense. If we have sexual relations for pleasure only, we usually feel empty and guilty. Also, if we have a relationship based only on caring and compassion, but without any sexual interest there is no balance either. It can also mean some kind of insecurity regarding your sexual performance; it is an alarm signal to get orientation by a sexologist who will help you to find your equilibrium.

Spirituality:	It shows that your senses of equality, equity, harmony and justice are balanced. It can happen that you occasionally feel that you are not sure about the spiritual path to follow. Justice indicates that you can discern which is the best way for you. Meditate (look for the instructions in the Meditation area) and the answer will come at the right time.
Profession:	It can indicate that you are going through a moment of doubts and that reflection and analysis are necessary to clarify them. You have to try to get a balance between your professional and your emotional life. It is important that in your work environment you cultivate empathy towards your co-workers and look for the best of each of them.
Goals:	It alerts us that it is unavoidable to achieve balance between what our purposes are in life so that the result can be as harmonious as possible. When you set your goals, analyze how they affect the other areas in your life. The appearance of this card can also suggests that you could dedicate yourself to a profession in the legal area. Explore which alternatives work for you.
Introspection:	It is a signal that equilibrium is missing. It is telling us that it is vital to travel inside ourselves, but it also alerts us that it cannot become an obsession. All excesses are detrimental to your mental and physical health.

XII

THE HANGED MAN
Challenges/Learning/ Surrender

The Hanged Man is a card of much learning. It teaches us to work on our insecurities, guilt, fears and shocking moments. We think that we cannot get out of the challenging situation we are in. However this card will teach us that if we devote to it, if we believe and trust in God, (the Universe, our Superior Being or how you want to say) everything is possible and any situation or conflict can be solved. When we render everything to our Superior Being and allow that She/He acts, the solution will come at the right moment.

This card alerts us that we have to pay a lot of attention to everything that happens around us. It is the moment when you are like floating in the air; the moment when there is a breakthrough to be able to connect and hold on to Divine Providence. It is the transition between one moment and another, the instant of total devotion and confidence in God. We surrender to the power of this force superior to us and we trust that whatever happens will always be for our greatest benefit and the wellbeing of everybody around us

When The Hanged Man appears in the area of:

Identity: It signals that maybe you are going through moments of much guilt. It is possible that you have many doubts and you do not know who you really are. During relaxed meditation you can ask yourself: who am I, and pay attention to the answers.

Finances: It means that you feel tied to your finances. You do not know which way or in what direction to go, nor how to solve your financial situation. It is necessary that you thank the Universe for all the possessions it gave you and that you ask for strength to administer them well. Go to the finances area and do the recommended exercises.

Mind: It reveals that you are at a time of transition. It is possible that you feel disoriented and that you do not know what action to take. Maybe you are going through a depression and it is necessary to look for the help of a psychiatrist. Daily meditation is absolutely necessary at these moments.

Home/Family: It can indicate that family relations are very vulnerable. Maybe there are moments when you want to run out, but you feel tied down and paralyzed. This cards gives us the opportunity to see the internal and external factors that are strongly influencing the environment of your home. The help of a professional counselor or a family psychologist is necessary.

Creativity/Fun: It denotes that Fun and Creativity are not your priority right now. However, after the areas of Spirituality, Mind, Individuality and Introspection, you have to attend them urgently. It is important to raise your energy, and the way you do that is feeling high frequency vibration emotions like love, joy and happiness.

Health: It is recommended to pay special attention to your mind and thoughts. Be careful with addictions.

Relationships: It can indicate that sometimes you do not trust anybody around you. You do not know if you are surrounded by friends or enemies. Maybe you feel in suspension and you do not know what to make of things. Maybe you feel guilty and it is necessary to forgive yourself and also those you feel have harmed you, so you can start new relationships. You can also restart your existing relationships with forgiveness and trust.

Sexuality: It can show that you feel tied down and paralyzed. You would like your sexual relation to be different, but when the moment comes you do not know what to do at that intimate and highly expected instant by you and your partner. If it is necessary get the help of a sexologist so you can transcend this situation.

Spirituality: It says that it is absolutely necessary to be aware of everything around us. It is the moment of total trust in our Superior Being. Spiritual practice (whichever you have chosen) is the balm you need today.

Profession: It suggests that you can be going through a moment of uncertainty. Maybe you are doubting that what you are doing is really what you are passionate about and want to do it for the rest of your life. Get the Meditative Coaching questions and answer them honestly to clarify what you feel.

Goals: It can indicate that you are not clear about what your goals are. There is confusion and disorientation at this instant. It is time to let go of what ties you down and look for new paths.

Introspection: Analysis and introspection are necessary. Internal working has to be done so you can get rid of the chains that tie you down. Always put God first in your life and everything else is going to develop little by little. Remember that everything passes, nothing is permanent.

XIII

DEATH
Transcendental/ Determining

Death does not exist. It is simply a transition. It is a deep change; it is the end of a phase and the beginning of another one. In any area the card comes up it indicates that the period we are living right now is coming to an end or has already ended, and it is our responsibility to make this change transcendental in order to obtain spiritual growth and a better quality of life.

It is a moment of deep transformation when it is necessary to prepare for what is approaching, maybe a new job, a new love or friends. Fertile ground is achieved by feeling happiness, gratitude and appreciation for everything that comes to our life.

Identity: Very deep changes will be happening to you. At this moment new ways of looking at life are necessary. It is a transcendental transition and it deserves analyzing and going deeper into all of the Mandala for Transformation areas. It is a call for adopting new ways of living.

Finances: It indicates that the end of a period is near. It is possible that times of great financial challenges are about to finish. It is necessary for you to analyze what happened in order to be able to start with a clear mind and trusting that God will give you the necessary instruments to establish an action plan and revitalize your finances.

Mind: It can mean the revival of your way of thinking. It is an internal and deep transformation where your concept of life, love, money and relationships will change totally. It is your responsibility that this change will be for the better.

Home/Family: It reveals that your home life is in total transition. It is absolutely necessary to take action so you can transform the relationship with your children and your partner. It is the moment to end old grudges and start from zero with a clear mind and a heart full of love. It can also mean that you have to be prepared to let go of things with love and compassion.

Creativity/Fun: It suggests that the period of apathy you may be experiencing is coming to an end. It is a call to take back the reins of your life and have fun, so your creativity emerges. The energy of happiness is very powerful, use it for your benefit. Pay attention to something new coming to your life that makes you enjoy yourself and ignites dormant creativity.

Health: It signals that a time of physical challenges may be coming to an end. It is also necessary to pay special attention to symptoms which undermine your physical health inadvertently. It can mean that the challenges which affected your health are psychosomatic. Focus on them and analyze your symptoms to be able to discern between physical and mental. This card suggests to you that once you discarded a physical situation you see a psychologist who can help you to detect emotional problems or situations.

Relationships: It means that your relationships (friends, co-workers and /or partner) are in a deep transformation process which will create a change of the way to deal with them.

Sexuality: Maybe you are experiencing a situation of sexual impotency or frigidity (in case of women). If this is the issue consult a professional for help. It can also mean a deep transformation of the sexual relation with your partner. Dialog is unavoidable in these moments of transcendental changes so that both are satisfied with their results regarding sexuality.

Spirituality: It is an indication of a transcendental change in your spiritual life. Change will come, if you like it or not. It is the opportunity God gives you to step aside and let Divinity work in you.

Profession: It is a signal that one part of your professional life has ended and a new cycle is beginning. Maybe it is a change of job or profession. It can also indicate that it is time to change the way you have been doing things in your professional environment.

Goals: It reveals that it is a transition and transformation period. It is recommended that you evaluate your goals based on what you are living right now. It is time to let go of attachments and evolve.

Introspection: It can mean a transcendental moment of much transformation in your life. It is a good time to begin anew, remembering that there is always a revival. The sun comes up every day and presents the opportunity to bloom into a new state of consciousness. Take advantage of it.

XIV

TEMPERANCE
Patience/Adaptation/Reflection

Temperance personifies patience, adaptation, prudence and discipline we must have to reach the goals we have set for ourselves.

It proposes a time of reflection in order not to make decisions abruptly. It suggests to us to be watchful and alert in order to act with prudence at the right moment. This card represents a time to move away from the situation so you can analyze it from the observer's point of view and you can adapt to the circumstances. In any area it comes up it means prudence, conciliation and calm.

If Temperance expresses itself in the area of:

Identity: It can alert that it is the moment to muster all your calm, good sense and sanity. It shows that you may be at a very serene period of your life and that all decisions you make must be evaluated with caution.

Finances: It alerts that it is time to be cautious with expenses. It is important to observe how and where you are investing money. There is a time for everything and this is the moment to save.

Mind: It can mean your need to withdraw and make time for yourself. It indicates that you have to get out of the situation to be able to look at it from an observer's point of view and not to be attached to it.

Home/Family: It reveals that your home life is in an observation period. It is necessary to do things calmly if you have any friction with your family members. Temperance tells you that it is important to make an intelligent evaluation of what happens in your home at this moment.

Creativity/Fun: Its shows you that maybe you are holding back your desire to have fun. Remember however that this card represents moderation. Allow yourself to have fun in moderation so you do not get into excesses, if that is your fear. That is how you can unleash your creativity.

Health: It suggests that you take care of your feet, knees and ankles. If a doctor has not ordered the opposite, walking would be recommended to you at these moments.

Relationships: It means that your relationships are at an observation stage. Evaluate their positive aspect and which ones can improve. Maybe it is a good moment to take sometime for yourself and analyze what you and the others contribute to your life.

Sexuality: It indicates that you are putting a brake on your sexuality. It can show the absence of passion. If this is the case look inside and ask yourself if you feel passion for your partner. If you do not, maybe it is the moment to detach yourself and let go. It can also reveal that now is the time to reevaluate the pros and contras of the relationship.

Spirituality: It indicates that you are in a phase of quieting down. One of the Tai Chi precepts tells us that sometimes the best movement is no movement. This card alerts that it is time for analysis, reflection and prayer.

Profession: It can signal that it is time to take a break and reflect about the next movement. It means that there is a rhythm to everything and that it is necessary to wait the appropriate time to act. Temperance urges you to be patient with your co-workers on the job. This card asks you to make good use of your skills and use your harmony to help others.

Goals: It shows that you have to take advantage of this moment to carefully observe what your goals are. Maybe you had moments of doubt when you thought of changing course. Temperance shows you to move harmoniously and how to flow with the situations that can come up on the way to reach your goals.

Introspection: It reveals that it is a time of much reflection. This card reminds you that patience and perseverance are essential to continue the journey. Success means enjoying the trip. Work on yourself and do not be afraid, trust God above all things and pray to be in harmony with the Protective Forces of the Universe.

XV

THE DEVIL
Bewildering/Confusion/Resistance

The Devil card represents our dark side, our shadow. It means unawareness and the passions that ties us down. It indicates an unconscious desire to control others. It is the egotist part of our being, ire and impotence which are felt when we cannot change things the way we want. This card can indicate that if we do not recognize egotism and fears they can become barriers for our mental, emotional and spiritual development.

The Devil card challenges us to confront our fears and "take the bull by the horns" to work on a new state of consciousness. It alerts us about a compulsive, obsessive and addicted personality.

In any area it shows up it brings our fears, obsessions, hang ups and weaknesses to the surface to expose them to the light of our consciousness.

It gives us an opportunity to open our eyes, tell our story, resolve the conflicts and let this interior light we have illuminate the darkness of our shadow and help us to put them in harmony.

When The Devil card appears in the area of:

Identity:
It can indicate that you are letting yourself be guided by instincts and not by your intuition or your heart. It is the moment to bring up all your fears and confront them. When you put them in their place you can get rid of them and free yourself.

Finances:
It can show that you have an exaggerated attachment to money. It also alerts you that the obsession to have more money could become the axis of your life.

Mind:
It signals that you have to pay attention to addictions (sex, people, food, alcohol, drugs). Watch your behavior and if necessary see a psychologist or visit a support group immediately. It can also indicate that your energy for objective thinking is very low.

Home/Family:
It shows that there are hidden situations to be resolved. It alerts you that you should not take a controlling attitude trying to arrange things your way to get your wishes. Do not judge and learn to value your family members' opinions.

Creativity/Fun:
It alerts you to avoid excesses when having fun. Make sure that you did not get too deeply into exaggerated patterns of alcohol-, cigarette- and/or any other kind of drug consumption. If your body is intoxicated, creative energy does not manifest itself. This could take you to a state of severe depression.

Health:
It suggests that you attend to your genitals and your elimination system (intestines and rectum).

Relationships:	It can mean that you want to control all your relationships. You want people to act the way you like it. Maybe you have a compulsive desire to try to control the people around you.
Sexuality:	Maybe it indicates that you can be obsessed with your partner to an extend that you do not let him/her breathe. True love is unconditional and free. The desire to control clouds understanding.
Spirituality:	It indicates that there is a spiritual struggle inside you. This is a good moment to go back to your spiritual practice. It is recommended that you pray consistently; that you start and end your days praying.
Profession:	It can show that you feel you work too much for only little money. However it can also mean material success and apparent triumphs, because there is an emptiness inside you that you have not been able to fill.
Goals:	It is the moment to review your goals. This card calls your attention to the fact that in order to achieve them it is not necessary to deceive, trample on, mistreat or dominate others. The sweet taste of triumph is obtained when we worked harmoniously with others and the result is that everybody wins.
Introspection:	It recommends to you that you write down your story and re-write your novel. When you write it, use the present tense and express the details about how you want your new life to be. Finish with an acknowledgement and appreciation paragraph with all the good things in your life right now. Acknowledge that your shadow – or dark side - has had a purpose in your existence and that you can use this low vibration frequency energy in a healthy way.

XVI

THE TOWER

Albert Einstein said: *"We cannot solve problems with the same thinking we used when we created them."* The Tower card indicates reconstruction; doing things in a different way. It proposes that we redo the situation in a creative way.

This card also alerts to changes as well as unexpected and surprising events and that we have to make the respective readjustments. In any area it comes up it means reconstruction and it suggests a different way to act to be able to achieve our purposes. It is a transcendental card because the changes are unexpected and surprising. They are neither good nor bad and the way you receive them will depend on how you interpret them. It is good to remember that challenges are the contrast that helps us to value the blessings the Universe has given us.

You have to focus your attention on the area where this card appears because it generally indicates a moment of intense challenge.

If The Tower appears in the area of:

Identity:
It can indicate that you are going through a moment of reconstruction and reevaluation of your values and your way of looking at life. Maybe your are going through an existential crisis where you question everything in your life. It is a good opportunity to work on changing what does not satisfy you.

Finances:
It can show that you are in a financial crisis. It is the right moment to change the way you use and save your money. Make an action plan to honor your financial commitments.

Mind:
Focus on your mental process and observe your mind. Try to calm your thoughts using the meditation techniques suggested in this book. This card can show the coming on of a nervous crisis. It also indicates that you have to take the reins of your life back. Even if it seems that everything has ended it can be the beginning of a new and better existence.

Home/Family:
It alerts that you may be confronting very challenging moments. Maybe a family conflict could happen. It is important that you see it as a blessing because sometimes behind what we consider a problem a blessing is hiding. Take your time to observe and discover the gift that this unexpected change brings you.

Creativity/Fun:
It shows that you are urgently looking for different ways to have fun and to use your creativity. You have to attend to this area immediately so you can balance the rest of the areas of your life. During this time reflect about what Albert Einstein said: *"Imagination is more important than knowledge."* So use it to create new ways to have fun.

Health: You have to dedicate special attention to your nervous system. This card alerts that it is necessary for you to do all the tests recommended by your trusted doctor. Pay attention to body signals so you can act immediately.

Relationships: It can mean that your relationships go through a reconstruction period. It is necessary for you to observe the motive of the changes and to work on renewing relationships, be it with a partner, friends or at work.

Sexuality: It signals that you expect the unexpected. That means that anything can happen in your sexual relation. It is a good moment to reconstruct the intimacy with your partner and make love in a different way. Maybe it would be something surprising and nice to put a little humor into the relation.

Spirituality: It represents a call for the change you have to make in your spirituality. It is a total turnaround. It could be a time of destroying all dogmas and old structures that you feel are tying you down and do not let you stay united with Divinity. It is a call for the transformation of your spiritual life. It is a good moment to study some life philosophy that is within your own energy vibration.

Profession: It can indicate a moment of unexpected changes in your profession. It is time to take a good look at what it is you are doing and if it agrees with your purpose in life.

Goals: This instant is ideal to reconstruct and set new goals for yourself. Keep calm when unexpected changes could occur. It is important to use them in your favor. Your spiritual practice is the instrument that will help you at these moments.

Introspection: It can indicate that you will have to reorganize your life to experience the calm after the storm. It is the moment to get on top of the wave of change to be able to get to shore safely.

XVII

THE STAR
Faith/ Hope/Inspiration

This card represents dreams, projects for the future, ideals. It can indicate that when we have faith and pay attention to positive feelings like: love, happiness, appreciation, peace, joy and gratitude we will have great possibilities to make our goals come true. These feelings increase energy vibration and help us to connect to the Divine Energy around us to bring all we long for to manifestation.

In any area this card comes up it indicates that we have to believe in God and in ourselves. It means the progress of projects we are accomplishing when we take the necessary action to make them become reality.

If this card comes up in the area of:

Identity:
It can show that you look at life with hope and joy. Be careful however not to be too idealistic because that can make you live a little out of reality. This card also advises you to cultivate the quality of discretion.

Finances:
It indicates that you need more maturity and knowledge about how to invest and save your money. It is the right moment to get educated about the way to manage your finances, which will help you to make informed decisions regarding your money.

Mind:
In this area it can show that it is necessary that you work on your mind in order to achieve high vibration thoughts like love and compassion. Meditation and your spiritual practice are the instruments that help you to increase your energy vibration. A positive attitude towards life will make you transcend any situation you are confronting right now.

Home/Family:
It exhorts you to use the power of love irradiating from your heart. This will help to you achieve the objectives of peace, harmony and happiness you want to accomplish in the environment of your home. This card shows that you are loyal, faithful and that you have a clear concept about what you want for the benefit of your family.

Creativity/Fun:
It suggests that you love to play and have fun, even if sometimes you put a brake on your emotions. This card urges you to enjoy what you have, to let your creativity flow, to enjoy yourself and forget about what others might say.

Health:	You have to specially focus on your intestines. This card recommends to you that you increase fruit and vegetable intake to activate peristaltic movement.
Relationships:	It means that there is a certain degree of immaturity in your relationships. This card shows that you are loyal, faithful, confident and that you tend to idealize people, which sometimes makes you suffer deceptions.
Sexuality:	It signals that sometimes you hold back your feelings. Occasionally you can be a little uncommunicative with words, because you believe that actions speak louder than a thousand words. However sometimes it is good to express what you feel at the moment you make love.
Spirituality:	It represents a sensation of inner peace. It is this union with God that makes it easier to reach your goals. It is the unbreakable faith you have in the Almighty and you know that with God everything is possible. It represents unconditional love between Divinity and you.
Profession:	It indicates that you like what you are doing right now. You love your profession and this love will make all your dreams come true.
Goals:	It can indicate that this is the moment to fight with faith for everything you aspire to. Inspiration and creativity will give you the necessary push to achieve your goals.
Introspection:	It symbolizes a state of hope where you have faith in your relationship with the Universal Forces. The appearance of this card indicates that you have to help yourself and remember that the answer is always within you.

XVIII

THE MOON
Doubts/Uncertainty/ The Unknown

In general terms this card can mean fears, doubts, uncertainty, the subconscious and the unknown. It is a card that represents challenges, but it also shows us the intuition we possess to transcend them.

It can represent insecurity and in some way it confronts us with our hidden fears. It alerts us that occasionally those fears can be exaggerated. The appearance of The Moon in a spread is a call to bring fears to the light of consciousness in order to heal old wounds.

It can also mean a great intuition which we have to use for the well-being of others and our own, because when we feel good it has repercussions on the people who share our life. It is our inner voice calling for our improvement and to bring out any shadow that we have in our subconscious.

In any area it shows up the card can mean exaggerated fears, transcendental challenges and a call for using our intuitive capacity wisely. It is a reminder that at these moments practicing meditation consistently is unavoidable for you.

It The Moon card comes up in the area of:

Identity:	It can symbolize that you are in a duality process. Probably you are between two waters and you do not know which way to go. Maybe you are mixed up and you cannot take all of the angles of the situation into consideration. It is absolutely necessary for you to meditate every day (look for the Meditation area on page 15) so you can bring light to all those dark areas in your life and increase your intuition. It will help you to see the path to follow more clearly.
Finances:	Maybe you are going through moments of much doubt, fears and uncertainties regarding your financial situation. You could confront an unstable but passing period of time. This card reminds you that nothing is permanent; believe in God, have faith and patience.
Mind:	It alerts you that right now you could be at a stage of bewilderment and confusion. Pay attention to the unconscious motivations that cause you to to act in a way that differs from the natural movement of the Universe. It is as if The Moon moved in the opposite order of the planets. Maybe you go through a period of compulsive and obsessive instability. It is even possible that this will literally not let you sleep. If even your moments of rest become affected it is recommended to see a psychologist you trust.

Home/Family: It indicates some disagreement in the family. At this moment you have to be very careful because you could have an emotional outburst that will take you to make hurtful comments which you really do not feel. The Moon intensifies emotions and it is necessary to let waters return to their level in order to sit down and negotiate.

Creativity/Fun: It can let you know that it is a little difficult for you to give yourself the freedom to express your creative abilities and have fun. It can also show a certain insecurity and unconscious fears that keep you from manifesting yourself in a creative way. You are too afraid of critics. Free yourself and let your creativity flow and enjoy it.

Health: Pay attention to this area. The Moon represents the reproductive organs: breasts, ovaries, the womb. They are not necessarily in a bad condition, but you have to pay attention to them. Due to the fact that The Moon rules feminine aspects it is recommended that you see a gynecologist and that you have all your tests up to date.

Relationships: It reveals some kind of deception regarding relationships, which could be with a partner, family or at work. Maybe you feel that someone has not been honest with you. Dialog is always good to clarify any misunderstanding. This card alerts about a damaging level of mistrust you must observe and work on.

Sexuality: It signals that you have hidden and unconscious fears regarding your sexuality. Many doubts come up about you sexual behavior and this could make it impossible for you to fully enjoy the relations. This card suggests you see a sexologist and that you explore your sexuality.

Spirituality: It can indicate that your intuition is at one of its best moments. The spiritual practice you have chosen is something you should experiment so you could learn to hear your inner voice better.

Profession: Maybe The Moon is taking you over very challenging ways. Unfounded fears, uncertainties and doubts can be the order of the day. It is absolutely necessary that you meditate on a daily basis to transcend the fears and challenges you could be living at these moments.

Goals: It can indicate that you are not so sure what it is you want to achieve in life. Maybe your goals are not clear to you, you do not have any planned objectives and you do not know which strategy to use to achieve them. The recommended action for the Goals (see page 156) is a good ally to help you clarify your doubts.

Introspection: It shows that internal work has to be done to get all the "skeletons out of the closet." It is necessary for you to make peace with your dark side and - with the help of techniques recommended in the book – bring any characteristic of your personality you want to change to the light.

XIX

THE SUN
Positive/Stimulating/ Encouraging

It is said that The Sun is one of the best Tarot cards. It is positive, stimulating and encouraging. It represents light, heat, clarity. Everything we see with the energy of the sun is clear, diaphanous and without folds.

So this card constitutes optimism, confidence, honesty, innocence of the heart and unconditional love.

It shows happiness, enjoyment and the triumph of love over all things. It means the satisfaction you get from having honored your values.

In any area this card comes up it indicates that the achieved success is due to the devotion you put into everything you do.

If The Sun comes up in the area of:

Identity: It says that you have a sociable personality and the ability to make people feel happy when they are around you. At this moment your experiences make it possible for you to see life in a happy and joyful way.

Finances: It can indicate that at this moment your financial situation is improving. It is a confirmation that money energy is moving in your favor. Take advantage of The Sun's high energy to create a savings and retirement plan that will give you long term benefits.

Mind: It signals that you are taking advantage of your intuition. Your interior dialog is clear and firm. Your mind is open to receive new information that helps you to harmonize feelings and reasoning. This cards recommends that you meditate consistently.

Home/Family: It can indicate that you have happy and harmonious relationships with all members of your family. Happiness comes from within and The Sun gives you the high vibration of love energy, so you can share it with everybody at home. This card suggests to you to plan activities where everybody in the family participates.

Creativity/Fun: It lets you know that you enjoy everything abundantly. Take advantage of this high energy vibration to create what you have been planning for a long time. Have fun doing what you like. This card predicts that everything you do at this moment will bear fruit that will give you much satisfaction.

Health: You have to pay attention to your circulatory system and The Sun represents the energy of the heart. That does not mean that you have a sick heart, but it can alert you to have the corresponding medical check-ups done.

Relationships: It indicates good relationships with your co-workers, friends and your partner. Take advantage of this energy for activities that foment these connections because the sun energy you bring to manifestation keeps it stable.

Sexuality: It can signal that you enjoy your sexuality to the maximum. It represents the satisfaction of love and friendship taken to the area of sexuality. It is total communication of a couple. It is an excellent moment to express what you feel, which will help you to identify with your partner.

Spirituality: It can suggest that your intuition increases every day. It is the moment to recognize that voice within you and act according to the information you receive. Your communication with God will give you satisfaction and you feel in peace.

Profession: It shows moments of triumph. You are reaping what you sowed with a lot of perseverance. This card is a confirmation that now you love what you are doing and that you enjoy your profession to the maximum. It is important that any task you start has the goal that everybody wins, so they all benefit.

Goals: It confirms that your goals are clear and that you know where you are going. The Sun gives you the necessary energy to pursue your goals. You have a clearly defined action plan which will help you to see any challenge that might come up from an observer's point of view without being tied to the results. This card suggests that you have very good possibilities to be successful due to your good planning.

Introspection: It indicates that you learned your lessons well. The Sun's energy helps you during your self-realization process. Your intuition is at its highest point and your spiritual energy has flourished, and now you reap the fruits of your internal work.

XX

JUDGEMENT
Transformation, Resurrection, Reflection

Judgement is the great pause which is necessary to reflect about our actions. It means stopping all actions and analyzing everything we have done up to now in order to make vital life changes. It represents a time where we transform all our believes in order to resurge to a new life and awaken to a new consciousness.

The energy of this card calls us to transform our life through reflection, analysis and meditation to be reborn.

In any area it shows up it indicates that it is absolutely necessary to stop and reflect, analyze and meditate in order to make the necessary changes and to achieve rebirth.

If The Judgement card shows up in the area of:

Identity:
It can indicate that there is much movement in your life. Maybe there will be new beginnings for you that will mean new challenges.

Finances:
It signals that at this moment your finances are changing fast. It is intelligent to review your investments, savings, life- and incapacity insurance; that means all your insurance policies. If you do not have any, this card alerts you about the need to get one. It is convenient to analyze the advantages to have all these insurance policies at the moment of a mayor eventuality.

Mind:
It suggests that you are thinking of many projects at the same time. It can alert that your mental buzz is very active and that daily meditation is necessary to quiet your mind down and to be able to concentrate on your projects; one at a time.

Home/Family:
Maybe it indicates that your family relationships are very active. They are in a transformation process. These changes can be very good or very challenging, it all depends on the situations that are happening and how they are being handled. Due to the fact that this card represents much movement it can mean that you had even thought of moving to another place. Judgement alerts you that you have to consider the opinion of all your family members before making such an important decision.

Creativity/Fun:
It says that you like activity. Dancing, practicing Yoga or Tai Chi and everything that takes movement is recommendable for you right now. Your creativity is surfacing, use it to improve all areas of your life with actions and thoughts.

Health: It represents the hormonal and analysis processes. Observe your thoughts and emotions. If you feel that your thought analysis process is affecting your feelings it could be necessary that you see your trusted doctor to work on your physical health and a psychologist to deal with your mental health.

Relationships: It can show that new friendships come to your life and that maybe it is time to let go of other ones. The relationship with your partner can be moving strongly, old feelings of love or rejection may come up. Make time to analyze and reflect about it. You have a great opportunity to transform the relationship with your partner. It is in your hands if this transformation is for improvement or good bye.

Sexuality: It indicates that your sexuality can be at a discovery moment for you and your partner. Maybe you are experimenting with new ways to make love which will help develop and strengthen it.

Spirituality: It means that your intuition is in full movement. This card gives you the opportunity to pay more attention to everything that happens in your life. You are in a spiral movement towards your interior evolution. Use this energy in your favor so you can activate your inner wisdom.

Profession: It presents a time of much movement; changes that help you to believe in your Superior Being and trust the wisdom of Divine Intelligence. It can mean an awakening of consciousness that will help you to know what you really want to do in your life.

Goals: It is a good moment to reflect about your goals and the path you want to follow. Judgement can represent this instant of decision when it is necessary that you are honest with yourself and evaluate what you really want to achieve. It is time to renew your attitude towards life and rethink the goals that honor the values according to which you decided to lead your life.

Introspection: It represents a cosmic wake-up call. Hand over the reins of your life to the cosmic forces of the Universe.

XXI

THE WORLD
Positive/Evolution/Active

The World card shows us the integration of all our experiences to use them in our spiritual growth. When this card comes up in any of the work areas, harmony of our body-mind-spirit is evident. It is necessary to take advantage of its energy to make a quantum leap in our personal and spiritual development.

The appearance of The World reminds us that we are responsible of our achievements and learning. It is also a reminder that we are the architects and not the spectators in our life. This card makes a call for our action which is needed to reap what we sowed. Additionally it indicates that it is necessary to keep a humble attitude regarding achievements so that the ego will not interfere with what we have accomplished.

In any area it appears it alerts us that there are new challenges to overcome and also new happiness to enjoy. It also signals to us that in order to develop the talents God has given us our evolution has to be active and dynamic.

If this card comes up in the area of:

Identity:
It can indicate that you are pleased with what you achieved as a human being. You feel satisfied about being the person you are at this moment of your life.

Finances:
It shows that you did a good job with money energy. It is a clear signal that you feel optimistic because you can see and enjoy the fruits of your efforts and the discipline you practiced.

Mind:
It describes that you have the potential to feel happy, confident, stable, secure with yourself and in harmony with everything around you. This card indicates to you that if you put your mind to it you can experience Yoga (union) and harmony with the Universe.

Home/Family:
It indicates that this moment is one of great harmony in your home. If that is not the case the appearance of this card confirms that you have full potential to achieve it. Activate your interior wisdom and act so you can manifest harmony, peace and balance in your family life.

Creativity/Fun:
It shows that you like to have fun and make the most of it. Your creativity is showing and it is easy for you to create works (dances, music, paintings, etc.) without taking into consideration what others might think about them. This card reminds you that the only thing that matters is that you let your creative energy of the Universe emerge.

Health:
You have to pay attention to the areas The World represents: red blood cells, head and face. If pain or inflammation is noted in any of these areas it is an exhortation to see your trusted doctor.

Relationships:	It can show that you have good friends who you can rely on. Your relationship as a couple is at an integration period from the physical, mental and spiritual point of view. If that is not the case, this card assures you that you have all the possibilities to achieve it if you use your intuition and listen to the voice of your Superior Being.
Sexuality:	It indicates strength and evolution in the relationship with your partner. Your sexual energy can be at its maximum expression. If it is not that way practice the Yoga poses recommended for this area during 21 days because you are at the right moment to move your sexual energy.
Spirituality:	It shows that your intuition is very active and your connection with God is present in all your actions. At these moments of strong connection everything flows harmoniously in your life.
Profession:	It can indicate success, accomplishment and rewards for all the work done and your perseverance. It can also anticipate that if at this stage you work with determination you will reap the fruit you sowed.
Goals:	It means that it is a good time to review your goals and make the necessary adjustments to finish what you have pending and/or set new ones. The World can represent their achievement, but this will only happen when you are completely sure that they are the true objectives you want to manifest.
Introspection:	It represents peace, quiet, balance and equilibrium you acquired through your joyful effort to know yourself better. This card indicates the evolution of your inner self. When The World shows up in the spread it is a good signal that you can recognize that you are at one with God.

RECOMMENDED POSES FOR EACH AREA

For Hatha Yoga practitioners:

Before starting the Yoga-Tarot session meditate at least ten minutes and define your intention for this practice. For example: if you want to work on the finances area, a good intention could be: *"I intend to increase my savings account and pay off my financial commitments."* It is important to affirm them aloud because the sound vibration helps us to materialize our dreams. Intention is determination of willingness to achieve a result.

Then get your mat and do the Sun Salutation pose (at least three repetitions). Remember to keep breathing and if you feel any discomfort with any pose, release it and get back to your initial position. The recommendation is that you repeat the indicated pose at least three times.

For Hatha Yoga beginners:

Before starting the Yoga-Tarot session sit down in the Easy Pose (Sukhasana), meditate for at least ten minutes and express your intention for this session. For example: if you want to work on the spirituality area, a good intention would be: *"I intend to have a full spiritual life."* Remember that intention is determination of willingness to achieve a result.

If you decide to do the pose on the floor and you do not have a yoga mat it is recommended that you buy one. If you feel any discomfort in any pose get up and sit down comfortably on a chair. Continue meditating and when you feel it is convenient start the recommended process. Do not forget that you decide the order of how you are going to experiment the process. In my case I discovered that what best works for me is: meditating, filling out the Mandala for Transformation, do the recommended yoga pose, cast the Tarot spread and see what my message is, get my journal and answer the Meditative Coaching questions, write the answers in my journal,saying my affirmations aloud, singing them, dancing them, and finally lie down in Savasana to do the visualizations.

Hatha Yoga practitioners and no practitioners:

If you are a Hatha Yoga practitioner, after finishing your routine (if you have already filled in the Mandala for Transformation, chosen the area you want to work on and integrated the recommended poses) take your journal and answer the Meditative Coaching questions of the area you work on. Then do the Tarot spread (see instructions on pages 24-26) and look for the meaning of the card you got on the pages provided for it (see pages 176-256). Write your affirmations in the journal, say -, sing- and recite them at least 10-15 times. Finish in Savasana (resting pose) and start the visualization process.

If you do not practice Hatha Yoga (before you start classes with a qualified teacher), sit down comfortably and meditate. The order could be: fill in the Mandala for Transformation, choose the area you want to work on, get your journal and answer the Meditative Coaching questions of the corresponding area. Do the Tarot spread following instructions from the section provided for it and look up the meaning of the card in the corresponding section to see the message Tarot has for you. Lie down in Savasana (resting pose) and start the visualization process When you think it is convenient (you are relaxed) and you clearly defined your intention, sit down and make your affirmations.

In case of advanced practitioners they can choose any pose shown on page 279. The postures that are outlined are recommended for beginners. Always listen to your body and if necessary, release the pose and get back to your initial position.

RECOMMENDED POSES FOR HATHA YOGA BEGINNERS

All standing poses start with Tadasana (The Mountain)

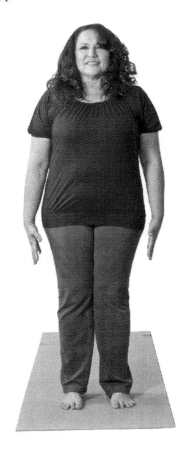

TADASANA

(Mountain Pose)

- Stand firm with your bodyweight distributed on both feet.
- Open your legs to the width of your hips.
- Mare sure your feet are parallel and pointing forward.
- Put your right hand on your belly button and the left hand on your sacrum.
- Move the sacrum backwards and then forward to be aligned with the spine (remember that it has a natural curve in the sacrum; do not force it to straighten it)
- Put your hands parallel to the body.
- Lift your shoulders, pull them back and down.
- The fingers have to point to the floor.
- Feel the energy flowing down your arms which are strong and firm.
- Feel the energy in your whole body.

AREA I –IDENTITY

Sukhasana (Easy Pose)

It is recommended that for this pose you fold one or two bath towels to a height of approximately 4 to 6 inches. Sit down at their edge with your legs extended in front of you. Inhale and exhale in a relaxed way during the whole process.

- Bend your right knee so that the foot is placed under the left knee.
- Bend your left knee so that the foot is placed under the right knee.
- If you want, when you start practicing the pose you can lean back against a wall
- At the end relax in Savasana (Resting Pose) and continue with the recommended process.

AREA II - FINANCES
Salamba Bhujangasana (The Sphinx)

Lie on your stomach

- Inhale and put your forearms on the floor. The elbows should be at the height of the shoulders, the arms are vertical and the hands are flat on the ground and the fingers are spread apart.
- Exhale and stretch your legs well; put all your energy into them.
- Inhale and lift your chest little by little. Continue inhaling and exhaling.
- When you finish relax in Savasana (Resting Pose) and continue the recommended process.

AREA III -- THE MIND

Adho Mukha Svanasana (Downward facing Dog) Modified

Get a chair, put it firmly against a wall and make sure it does not move.

- Stand in front of it in the Tadasana pose. (look for description on page 263). Inhale and lift your arms. When you exhale slowly bend down from the hip until you can put your hands on the chair.
- Your arms have to be at the height of your ears and the legs are straight. If this is difficult for you bend your knees slightly so you feel comfortable.
- Continue inhaling and exhaling and relax.
- To exit the pose, inhale and in exhalation bend your knees slightly, bend your back a little, take your hands off the chair and put them on the shins. If that is difficult for you put your hands on the knee.
- Inhale and slowly lift vertebra after vertebra until you are in the Tadasana pose again.

AREA IV – FAMILY

Tadasana with Flying Bird mudra

Stand in Tadasana

- Inhale and adopt the Flying Bird mudra, stretching out your arms at the height of the shoulders (in the shape of a cross).
- Your palms have to face upward.
- Extend your head backwards and be careful not to get your neck muscles caught.
- Lift your arms until they form a "v".
- Inhale and exhale slowly. Close your eyes and visualize what you want to happen in your family.
- When you finish relax in Savasana (Resting Pose) and continue the recommended process.

AREA V - CREATIVITY/FUN
Ananda Balasana (Happy Baby)

Lie on your back:

- Inhale and in exhalation bend your knees until they touch your stomach.
- Inhale and grab the inside of your feet.
- Exhale and open your knees wider than your torso.
- Align your ankles with your knees so that your shin is perpendicular to the floor.
  Continue inhaling and exhaling.
- Rest holding the pose.
- Inhale and in exhalation release the pose. Put your feet on the floor.
- Rest in Savasana (Resting Pose) and continue the process.

AREA VI – HEALTH

Savasana (Resting Pose)

Before you start roll a bath towel like a cylinder.

- Inhale and sit on the floor.
- Put the towel under your knees.
- To lie down on your back, bend your body down from the waist (each vertebra at a time) until your head reaches the floor.
- Spread your legs wider than your hips but still on the towel.
- Inhale and extend your arms wider than the body.
- Your palms have to face upward.
- Inhale and exhale deeply.
- Rest in this pose.
- Take advantage of it and do the Area VI: Health visualization.

AREA VII – RELATIONSHIPS
Virabhadrasana I (Warrior I)

Stand in Tadasana (Mountain Pose) (You can see the explanation on page 263)

- Inhale and in exhalation spread your legs about 4 feet with your feet parallel.
- Turn your right foot outward about 90 degrees.
- Turn the heel of your left foot inward about 10-15 degrees.
- Extend your arms outward in a cross position.
- Turn your torso to the right and look straight ahead.
- Lift your arms over your head. The palms of your hands face each other. Lower your shoulders and pull them back.

- Bend your right knee until it is perpendicular to your right foot and your shin is perpendicular to the floor.
- Keep the pose for as long as you can. I suggest that you do three breathings which will take about 15 seconds.
- Now repeat it on the other (left) side.

AREA VIII - SEXUALITY

Bhujangasana (The Cobra)

Lie on your stomach facing the floor.

- Inhale and put your hands on the ground. Make sure your fingers are at the height of your shoulders. Your elbows have to be pressed to your torso and your fingers are separated.
- Exhale and stretch your legs well, pressing your thighs and pubis area firmly to the floor. Put all your energy into this movement.
- Inhale and stretching your arms little by little, lift your torso from the floor until you feel at a comfortable height. Continue inhaling and exhaling focusing on the process. Observe the energy in your pubis and legs.
- The neck has to be extended in order not to strain the cervicals.
- Look straight ahead.
- The shoulders have to be pulled back so the sternum comes out a little.
- Keep breathing and remember that in case you feel uncomfortable, you can let go of the pose and go back to your initial position.
- Repeat the pose three times.
- Start the recommended process.

AREA IX – SPIRITUALITY
Ardha Padmasana (Half Lotus)

Sit down with your legs extended in front and the shoulders straight.

- Inhale and exhale. Bend your right knee until the sole of your right foot touches the inside of the left thigh.
- Inhale and exhale. Bend your left knee and put your foot on your right leg.
- The sole of the left foot must touch the inside of the right thigh.
- The ankle has to be on top of the right leg.
- Put your shoulders back so the spine is straight.
- Put your hands on your knees with the palms facing upward or downward, as you prefer.
- Repeat the pose on the other side (bend your left knee) and continue the process.
- Hold the pose for 30 seconds or one minute.
- Start the recommended process.

AREA X - PROFESSION/WORK

Vrkasana (The Tree)

Stand in Tadasana (The Mountain – see description on page 263)

- Put all your bodyweight on your feet.
- Inhale and transfer your bodyweight to your left foot.
- Exhale and lift your right foot until it is at a height of about three inches.
- When you feel comfortable with your balance, inhale and bend your right knee.
- Lift your foot until the sole touches the inside of you leftt thigh.
- Continue inhaling and exhaling. At the next inhalation put your hands together in a praying position. Your thumbs have to touch your chest.

- Release the pose during exhalation. Lower your arms and put your right leg on the floor.
- Repeat the pose on the other side.
- Start the recommended process.
- If it is difficult for you to stand on one foot, lean on the wall.

AREA XI – GOALS

Virabhadrasana II (Warrior II)

Stand in Tadasana (Mountain Pose) (See page 263)

- Inhale and in exhalation spread your legs about 4-5 feet (they have to be parallel)
- Turn your right foot 90 degrees outward.
- Turn your left heel 10-15 degrees inward.
- Inhale and in exhalation extend your arms in the form of a cross so they are parallel to the floor.
- Draw an imaginary line from heel to heel and make sure they are aligned.
- Bend your right knee until the thigh is perpendicular to the ankle.
- Make sure you knee is not turned inward or outward but aligned with the ankle.

- Keep your torso in the center of the body.
- Inhale, extend your arms outward even more. Exhale.
- Inhale and turn your head to the right, looking at your fingers.
- Try to hold the pose for 30 seconds.
- Repeat it on the other side.
- Continue the Yoga – Tarot for Transformation process.

AREA XII – INTROSPECTION

Child Pose

Inhale, kneel and if possible, sit on your heels.

- Exhale and rest your torso on your thighs.
- Inhale and if you can, put your forhead on the floor. If not, get a yoga block, fold a towel or use a cushion; put your forhead on it and rest your head comfortably without feeling any pressure.
- Exhale and extend your arms straight out in front, putting them firmly on the floor.
- Inhale and exhale. Relax in the pose the time your body resists it. Listen to your body, it is not necessary to extend the time very much. You will become stronger little by little and you will be able to hold the pose longer.
- To release the pose, inhale and lift your torso little by little, vertebra by vertebra. While you are doing this, look at your belly button until you sit again on your heels.
- Continue the Yoga – Tarot for Transformation process.

RECOMMENDED POSES FOR ADVANCED HATHA YOGA PRACTITIONERS

The following poses do not have any description or proceeding instructions and they are only recommended for people who have done them before and have been practicing Hatha Yoga for more than a year. If you do not have enough experience I recommend that you only practice with your qualified and certified Hatha Yoga instructor.

Area I	Identity	Padmasana
Area II	Finances	Bhujangasana or Dhanurasana
Area III	Mind	Salamba Sirsasana
Area IV	Home/Family	Ardha Chandrasana
Area V	Creativity/Fun	Prasarita Padottanasana
Area VI	Health	Savasana
Area VII	Intimate/Sexual Relations	Natarajasana
Area VIII	Sexuality	Eka Pada Rajakapotasana
Area IX	Spirituality	Balasana
Area X	Profession	Baddha Konasana
Area XI	Goals	Ustrasana
Area XII	Introspection	Paschimottanasana

Every journey starts with a small big step: The decision to undertake it.

When you make the decision to change in order to improve your life you are moving the Mandala for Transformation wheel and increasing the energy in all aspects of your life. When there is an energy movement the ego is going to look for ways to stay in the impasse it is in because it is its comfort zone.

During this work you are going to do, challenges and inconveniences may arise that make you consider if the change is worth it. At that moment you have to act with the consciousness of a person who wants to make the quantum leap which is liberation and decide to work on being happy independently of the circumstances that have to be faced. Pay special attention to them when they come up and consider them opportunities to go up one step on the Mandala for Transformation scale, which is nothing other than a quantum leap that gets you closer to your goals and objectives.

Look ahead, focus your attention on what you want to achieve and believe that the work you are doing is worth it. Trust that this joyful effort is going to bear the fruits you are expecting. Have faith in the Universe, in yourself and your capacities.

If however you relize you need help, look for a qualified professional (psychologist, mediator, psychiatrist, physician) to help you.

Free yourself to discover the immense potential within you and your true purpose in this life. Decide to be happy and live a full life with which you can contribute to improve our society and the whole world.

THE KEY TO YOUR HAPPINESS
Yoga – Tarot for Transformation

A methodology that guides you on your self-realization journey

This book presents a system that integrates yoga techniques, meditation, tarot, meditative writing, creative visualization, positive affirmations, coaching, Mandala for Transformation and the Action Plan. When you practice this method, energy moves in your favor and helps you to manifest everything you always desired and dreamt about.

The work will guide you in improving the twelve most important areas in your life:

Identity, Finances, Mind, Home/Family, Health, Creativity/Fun, Relationships, Sexuality, Spirituality, Work/Profession, Goals and Introspection.

The Key to your Happiness will help you to:

- Know yourself better
- Improve your finances
- Calm the mental buzz
- Develop harmonious family relationships
- Improve your health
- Awaken your creativity and have fun

- Build a healthy couple relationship
- Love your sexuality
- Construct a solid spirituality
- Overcome the fear of success

- Learn to set goals for yourself
- Discover the potential within you

Printed in the United States
By Bookmasters